Wednesdays with Barry

Wednesdays with Barry

Terry Amann

VANTAGE PRESS
New York

Published by Vantage Press, Inc.
516 West 34th Street, New York, New York 10001

Manufactured in the United States of America
ISBN: 0-533-14437-X

Library of Congress Catalog Card No.: 2002094362

0 9 8 7 6 5 4 3 2 1

To my children, Sarah and Rachel, and to my children's children . . . I wanted you to know . . . we tried to make the world a better place. . . .

The Spirit of the Sovereign Lord
is on me,
because the Lord has anointed me
to preach good news to the poor.
He has sent me to bind up the
brokenhearted,
to proclaim freedom for the captives
and release for the prisoners.

Isaiah 61:1

Contents

Foreword

Terry Amann is more than just my pastor and close friend. He is the man that helped me realize and answer my call from God to become a minister and a true brother in Christ.

This book is dear to me for many reasons. Barry Chubick, Jr. worked in one of the departments that I managed while I was at the Bunn-O-Matic Corporation in Creston, Iowa. He was a quiet, unassuming man and when I read about the murder in our local paper, I was stunned. Later, when Terry told me about the book idea, I was skeptical. He began to show me original transcripts and I knew they were from God. This story must be told.

The transformation that you are about to read is an extraordinary testimony to the power of God and His ability to change people's lives. Terry's passion for ministry, and especially jail ministry, made a profound impact on Barry and it is told on the following pages. Terry's partner in our local jail ministry, Pastor Jim McCutchan, a powerful man of God, accompanied Terry on this journey. Between these two men, and God's almighty grace, Barry Chubick, Jr. is no longer the man that was arrested for the tragic murder of his girlfriend a few years ago. This book is not written to glorify any of the people contained within the story. It is an affirmation to the glory and almighty grace of God, and a witness to the wonderful salvation power of Jesus Christ.

May God bless you and touch you as you read this amazing journey of tragedy, rescue, and grace.

—Tracy Edwards
August 2002

Acknowledgments

Special thanks go out to Barry Chubick, Jr. for allowing his story to be told; to Pastor Jim McCutchan for all he did with this project and for all that he does in ministry; to John Nasko, who directed the passion of this story into a readable work; to my wife Susan for her patience and prayers; and the Prayer Warriors at the First Presbyterian Church in Creston, Iowa.

Other persons who contributed to this book are: Don and Pat Hall; Scott Crosier; Alice Crosier; Roger Saxton; Deb Norman; Dorie Shiltz; Tom and Allison Danilovich; Tracy and Cindy Edwards; Pat Henry; Sue Teutsch; Tim Kenyon; Linda Walling; Marion James; SWRP; Betty Nixon; Jerry Nurnberg and Cindy Rippenger.

Introduction

My colleague in ministry, Jim McCutchan, and I began our jail ministry in Creston, Iowa, against the backdrop of the constant demands of being local church pastors. We each have our respective churches and their impossible schedules so we didn't have time for yet another ministerial commitment. However, Jim and I have both long felt called to another level in God's work by the "Biblical jail" mandates of Isaiah 61:1, Matthew 25:36, and Hebrews 13:3.[1] Whenever God calls persons, they can try to hide as Jonah did, or they can simply answer the call. We chose to answer.

Pastor Jim and I do want to make the world a better place. Still, we did not expect a dramatic shift in the human condition through our labors. We just set out to try to provide a ministry of presence for people who found themselves caught up in the criminal justice system in our little corner of southwestern Iowa. In the "ministry of presence," an ambassador for Christ enters a human drama with compassion and the willingness to listen. If the characters in the drama have fallen away from God, there is the hope of leading them back to God. If the characters don't know God, there is the possibility of letting them meet God. So we quietly went about our ministry. Soon after we got started, there was a murder in our community.

In the early morning hours of February 6, 2000, Jane Ruby, age forty-five, was brutally stabbed. She would be rushed from her home over to the Greater Community Hospital in Creston. Soon afterward, she died there. Her daughter, Dana Ruby, age twenty-three, was brought to the same hospital with stab wounds to the hand and thigh. By the end of the day, a male suspect, who was the live-in boyfriend of Jane, Barry Chubick, Jr., thirty-five, was arrested. He was charged with first-degree murder. On the following Wednesday, February 9th, I met Barry for the first time. Jim would meet him the following week.

Over the next several months, Barry, Jim, and I would meet on Wednesday afternoons from 2:00 P.M. until 3:00 P.M. Most of the time it would be one of us with Barry. On other days it would be all three of us meeting together, but there was also someone else there. The Holy Spirit was always present. Consequently, something dramatic happened over the course of those meetings. Barry started out angry, confused and bitter, but he came to embrace the Christian faith with passion and conviction. During this process, Jim and I were privy to the inner workings of the Holy Spirit upon an individual. What we realized toward the end of our time together was that the New Testament story of Paul's Letter to Philemon was being lived out right before our eyes. In that letter, the Apostle Paul befriends a slave named Onesimus while they are both in prison. The slave becomes a different person over the course of their incarceration. Paul sends Onesimus back to his master with confidence that the slave who Paul says was, "useless to you but now he has become useful both to you and to me."[2] The Apostle Paul became a father to Onesimus and Onesimus became a child to Paul. The father nurtured the son until he was ready to be sent on to his next station to lead a Godly life. Our relationship with Barry developed in the same manner. When it came time for us to let Barry go on his way, it felt the same as if a young adult were leaving the family home in order to make his way in the world.

There is a book that was written in 1997 entitled *Tuesdays with Morrie* by Mitch Albom. This is a beautiful story, which tells how a middle-aged man relearns the most precious moments of life by way of his former college professor who was dying from amyotrophic lateral sclerosis (ALS). *Wednesdays with Barry* does not seek to copy that book. Rather, in a way, it complements it. When we meet Barry Chubick, Jr., he is dying a spiritual death. It is a death sentence that has the potential to plague him for eternity. But unlike the professor dying a physical death, Barry has a chance to stop his spiritual death in its tracks, and then reverse it. He can do it through the name of Jesus Christ. This is a powerful story about how a person consumed in the depths of sin can undergo spiritual transformation. It is also a story of how two ministers, who witnessed this conversion, will be forever touched by grace through the power of the Holy Spirit. We stand humbled as witnesses to Barry, who has become a modern-day Onesimus stepping out of the pages of Paul's Letter to Philemon from prison. It is also a look at life behind the confines of the brick walls and the iron bars of a jail cell. It is a testament to the power of words in the form of hand-written letters. *Wednesdays with Barry* is a book that puts America on notice that there is a better way to face the moral failures of our society. There is a better way that can be accomplished with spiritual compassion and direction. Finally, this book is a true life story, with many tears . . .

Wednesdays with Barry

1

The People Gather for Worship

You shall not murder.

—Deuteronomy 5:17

The country is trying to grapple with a presidential election that has been stumped by "Fuzzy's Math Theorem." Inside the Union County Courthouse building, court is in session. Barry Chubick, Jr. has already signed a plea bargain for second-degree murder. The courtroom is almost full. We are all gathered for the sentencing. I can hear people sniffling through tears from several groups behind me. There have been three surprises in the courtroom. Now, I am walking toward Barry. His hands and arms are not shackled. He reaches back with his left hand to mine. I am not sure that the judge will allow me to touch him. In an instant, I decide I need to. Our hands clasp. I realize that after all these months we have had together it is the first time that Barry and I are close to one another without any cell bars between us. Barry smiles. He is fighting back tears.

It is Sunday morning, February 6, 2000, in Creston, Iowa. The time is 6:30 A.M. Creston Police Officer Pat Henry has been up all night on the lonely 11:00 P.M. to 7:00 A.M. shift. He is thinking about getting home to get some sleep. Eight minutes later the police dispatcher's voice crackles over the squad car radio. Officer Henry is directed to go immediately to the emergency room at the Greater Community Hospital. Creston Police Officer John Sickels is already there. Sickels is talking with Dana Ruby. She is sitting on the floor in the hallway. In his role as a trained professional, Officer Henry makes a mental note of everything he sees and hears. Dana has blood on her pants because of a laceration to her left thigh. She is very upset. Directly behind Dana, in one of the hospital emergency rooms, lies Dana's mother, Jane. The emergency room staff and EMTs are administering CPR to her. Officer Henry's first thought is that *It doesn't look good in there.*

He talks with Dana to find out what happened and makes his report. He hears talk amongst the medical teams about calling in the Life Flight to get Jane to a Des Moines Hospital. Officer Henry leaves the hospital and heads over to 510 North Cherry, where the alleged crime has taken place. A description of a suspect is put together. The Cherry Street address is being secured as a crime scene and warrants are being sought for permission to enter and search the house for evidence. A short time later, the police are informed that Jane Ruby has been pronounced dead as a result of injuries from a stab wound through her back. Officer Pat Henry is now working a double shift on a murder case. The Department of Criminal Investigation (DCI) for the state of Iowa is called in to work with the Creston police to solve the case.

A few hours later, at 9:15 A.M., about a mile and a half away, Bible study class is just beginning. I am teaching the adult students. There are thirty six of us, ranging in ages from nineteen to eighty five. We are slowly making our way through the Gospel of John. Each class begins with a prayer. Then a student, who volunteered the previous week, brings in one or two topics of current events. Sometimes the topics tie directly into the lesson for the day, and sometimes they do not. We then engage in the Biblical text. I ask for a volunteer to read a section, and we begin to examine it, piece by piece. I do not use canned study lessons, preferring to write my own materials. I rely heavily on asking pertinent questions about the text at hand, coupled with self-discovery. During most of these study times we have lots of fun and laughs. Sometimes, we are simply all business. Down the hall from us, the children's Sunday school classes are under way with twenty eight young children ranging in age from three to fourteen. Forty minutes into the adult class members of the choir begin to leave. They gather with other choir members in the Red Room to practice before services begin. At 10:14 A.M. I ask for a volunteer to be the hunter-gatherer for current events the following week. I ask for another volunteer to close us with prayer. We disperse, and I begin to make my way to my office to the east of the church sanctuary. People stop me to give me prayer concerns. There is some talk about a domestic dispute that took place earlier in the morning and ended in murder. The details were very sketchy. Other people are still streaming in. Worship at the First Presbyterian Church of Creston, Iowa is set to begin at 10:30 A.M.

I have been with this congregation for almost a year and a half. We are part of the larger Presbyterian Church (USA). Last year we took in twenty-six new members, which is healthy growth for a small Iowa town with a declining population. So far this year we have received 15. We usually have about 120 people for worship. This morning our message is built around the 40th chapter of Isaiah. The title of the sermon is *"If we could just hit the rewind button of history."* It is a message about how random events can alter our lives forever. It is also a message about events in our lives that we wish we could change,

3

but we cannot. The topic came about because the community is reeling from a recent tragic auto accident that claimed the lives of five people; four of them Mormons, east of town on Highway 34, just a week earlier. On Sunday afternoon I learn of the irony of the sermon message, in light of the murder had taken place in the early morning hours that day.

Across town, on the south side of the tracks, Pastor Jim McCutchan begins his Sabbath morning ritual. He is up at 5:45 A.M. for devotional time. At 7:00 A.M. he turns the television on and watches a program called *Religion and Ethics*. His breakfast is coffee, toast and oatmeal. By 7:50 A.M. Pastor Jim climbs into his black 1976 Chrysler Cordoba. Like him, the car is a bit of a classic. He drives over to Wyoming Avenue and parks by the Assembly of God Church where he has been pastor for nine years.

From 8:00 A.M. until 9:00 A.M. Jim is in prayer, followed by a small break. At 9:25 he is joined by eight other men in his church from a discipleship group known as Honor Bound. They pray together for five minutes. Afterward, people head for Sunday School. Pastor Jim roams around, visiting the various classes. The service begins at 10:35 A.M. On this day, approximately a hundred people gather for worship and praise. One quarter of them are children. Worship opens with a prayer followed by announcements. The congregation is reminded that they will have a special guest, the Rev. Norman E. Wenig, on Valentine's Day. After announcements are completed, there is the morning collection. Then, electric guitars and piano, along with drums and singers are "turned loose," as Jim calls it. The pastoral message starts at 11:25 A.M. Pastor Jim preaches for thirty minutes. Worship closes with an altar call to see if anyone at worship would like to come forward to receive Jesus Christ into their hearts.

The Pentecostal worship service stands in great contrast to the more traditional form of worship in the Presbyterian Church.

Pastor Jim goes home after the service and attempts to get an afternoon nap. He needs the rest because the congregation will be back for an evening service. On this day, Pastor Jim returns to the church by 5:00 P.M. to pray. As he prays for the worship and praise service that is scheduled to begin at 6:00 P.M. there is a knock on his office door. Peggy Miller, the women's ministry leader, has disturbing news—there was a murder in Creston very early that morning. Jim informs his flock during the announcements that Jane Ruby is dead, and her daughter Dana is wounded. Many in his congregation knew the family. A pall then hangs over the rest of the evening service.

The Assembly of God Church learns what the rest of our community is also discovering—as our two respective churches, and the other area churches were doing the Lord's work today, all was not well in our town. Even though murder is not frequent, in Creston, Iowa, this would be the fourth domestic homicide here in a decade.[3] And despite its moniker as "Little Chicago" from days gone by, Creston is a wholesome town. It is a place that eight thousand residents call home. We are nestled around train tracks, which divide the town between north and south and are surrounded by farms made up of green valleys. There is a junior college, a YMCA, a couple of parks, and a Wal-Mart.

About twelve hours later, Barry Chubick, Jr. is arrested. He has been on the run and was actually in the process of returning to Creston through Ottumwa, Iowa. There, Barry runs a red light. When the Ottumwa police discover that Barry is wanted for murder, they arrest him on the spot. It is there, in the back seat of a squad car, that Barry learns of Jane's fate. His initial thought is, *Oh God, no! I can't believe it. I can't live, and don't want to live without her. I love her with all my heart. I would never do anything like that to her.* Almost two months later, Barry Chubick, Jr. enters a plea of "not guilty" to the charge of murder in the first-degree, and willful injury at the Union County Courthouse.[4]

2

The First Wednesday

You deserted the Rock, who fathered you;
you forgot the God who gave you birth.
—Deuteronomy 32:18

One of the best kept secrets we have around our part of the state is the man-made lakes. Jim and I like to fish. On rare occasions we can steal some time and go fishing together. We sit in Jim's boat. He is a far better fisherman than I. For every fish I get, he reels in five. I look across the sixteen-foot fishing boat at his face. Jim has deep green eyes, like those of a panther, sliding back and forth sweeping the top of the water. I am convinced he is reading the ripples of the lake looking for prey like a human radar. We are becoming close friends. We talk about a variety of topics, and we talk about Barry. Jim muses that it may be a while before Barry is able to fish in the boat with us even though there is enough room. Barry is looking at too much time behind bars. Jim casts another line. I take a swig of hot coffee. My affection for coffee is legendary. The awesome serenity of nature is all around us. Jim pulls another small bass into the boat.

Jim and I had only been coming up to the jail for a couple of weeks. We had met, for the first time, a year earlier at a prayer meeting. As we talked over the course of the next several months, we discovered we shared the same sense of call to do God's work behind cell bars. Jim had been praying for seven years for God to send other ministers to our town who had a passion for jail ministry. We discussed possible ways to go about setting up a ministry in our local county facility. Thus, as the world turned over into the new millennium with great hope, we set out to provide a ministry of presence, to those in need of some hope.

On February 9th, the first Wednesday that I met Barry, Jim was out of town on church business. Driving over to the jail, I thought how unfortunate it was that Pastor Jim was away. It was now three days since the murder. What if the murder suspect agreed to talk to me? What would I say? What would I ask him? After all, it had been seven years since I had done significant jail ministry. In fact, about the time I had finished at the Cook County Jail in Chicago, Pastor Jim started praying for a colleague with jail interests to come to Creston. I said a little prayer as I parked my car. I walked up the concrete stairs to the Union County Jail, and I could feel the same rush I used to get whenever I went into a larger prison. I noticed a crack in the stairs about halfway up. I walked past the police dispatcher's room where a couple of police officers were talking. They didn't look up. I took the claustrophobic elevator up to the second floor. The elevator door opened into a small section with the door to the jail immediately on my left. I pounded on this steel barrier. A petite woman in her middle twenties named Dorie Shiltz answered the door. She told me that the murder suspect was there. Dorie said she would ask him if he would like to see a chaplain. Her jail keys clanged and jingled as Dorie opened another steel door and disappeared behind it. She returned and informed me, "Chubick says he would like to talk with you." Dorie had two separate areas to watch over. Despite her small frame, she did not seem in any way intimidated by her choice of employment. On any given day, there might be about ten inmates locked up. Overwhelmingly, the cases of the accused in this jail revolve around drugs.

I could sense from the look on Dorie's face that she was concerned about the suspect as I went through that same steel door into a small, dark corridor. Dorie stepped away and left the door to the cell area slightly open. I turned towards the cell to peer in through the bars. Barry Chubick, Jr. was sitting on the bed. He was wearing dark blue jail-issue clothes. His feet had jail-issue sandals, which were an ugly bright orange. Barry dangled them over the edge of the bed. His hair was shoulder length and messy. His face bore a rough five o'clock shadow. His dark brown eyes almost bulged out of the sockets. His body was shaking uncontrollably. The cell area smelled like acrid smoke. The three walls of powder blue paint that surrounded him in the cell were chipped. The light was very dim. We looked at each other intently for about five seconds. Finally, I reached through the bars to shake hands. Barry stepped off the bed quickly and came over. He gave me a tight handshake as we exchanged names. He retreated back to the bed and sat down at a point in the cell that was farthest from me. His body continued to tremble. His new dwelling consisted of a stainless steel commode with sink attached. A small mirror bolted to the wall had long ago lost most of its reflecting power. The bunk was six foot long and only two-and-one-half-feet wide. The mattress was very thick, and the cover was all tattered. There was one blanket and no pillow.

I was surprised that Barry received me so well. I knew there was a possibility he might say something like, "Hey, I don't need any Bible thumper right now." That kind of reaction would have set our relationship way back, right from the beginning.

Months later, Barry recalled for me that first meeting. After our brief introductions, he had sensed that I knew he was hurting in a big way. I had asked Barry "simple questions," as he put it. For instance, I had wanted to know what sports he played. Barry had played football. That was an early victory for us, because I had wanted to make some connections or bridges with him right away. I had played nine years of tackle football, including a year of college ball, so I figured we could make some ground on this topic. Barry thought that I asked these simple questions to try to calm him down a bit. He was right.

So, at that first encounter, we went on through some more general questions. Barry remembered what was going through his mind during that first meeting. He said, "I kept telling myself, why does this guy even care about me? He doesn't even know me. The newspapers are portraying me as a murderer . . . But I could tell this guy cared about me. Yes—me!"

That first hour went by very quickly as we spoke in quiet tones. I tried to sound positive about the time that we might have together in the near future. At least twice, I was able to get Barry to smile. When it was time to go, I asked him if it would be okay to offer a closing prayer. Barry said it would be fine, and so I led us in a petition, in which I asked God to watch over Barry, and to speak to him in new ways. Then I thanked God for giving us the opportunity to meet.

As I got up to leave, I told Barry that my colleague Pastor Jim and I had hoped to see him next week. In jail ministry, you never promise an inmate anything. A visit to a prisoner can be as valuable as a bar of gold. They will often 'hang on' until the day arrives. Thus, if for some reason you cannot make it on the prescribed day, the inmate may become spiritually crushed. And as a minister to the jailed, you have lost your credibility for a broken promise. Consequently, I was careful not to promise Barry a return visit. Instead, I told him I would 'try' to be back with Pastor Jim the following Wednesday. I had said the phrase, "I will try to . . ." so many times at the Cook County Jail in Chicago that it rolled off my tongue as if it were part of my name. I gave Barry my business card and told him that if he needed to see me for something special between then and Wednesday, to ask one of the jail staff to contact me. We shook hands again. Our eyes did another assessment of one another. I understood later that, at that moment, we were having a silent conversation about our mutual destiny, but neither one of us had realized it at the time.

I turned and walked out of the cell area into the jail lobby or "intake section." Dorie was there to let me out as she prepared for a shift change. The large steel door closed with a thud. More barriers now separated Barry and me. Dorie turned the metal lock with the jail keys, and I could hear the interior latches catch as metal turned against metal. Dorie politely asked if it all went well. I told her it did. I also told her that I was concerned about the way Barry was shaking and seemingly still in shock. My fear was that he might try to take his own life. She said the jail staff was also very concerned about that possibility, so they had been watching him carefully. She unlocked the large steel door so I could leave the jail area. Once outside I took a deep breath. I was done with jail time for a week, while Barry was just beginning to try to make sense of his situation in a small, dark jail cell.

I began to wonder where to begin when I caught up with Jim. When we talked later in the week on the phone,

Jim wanted to know, "Were there any signs in Barry that you think we may have something to build on?"

"Yes, we definitely have some possibilities," I said.

Jim was pleased with that news. Then he reflected on the fact that we had another murder victim of domestic violence, "Dear Jesus, we have so much jail work to do out there and it's just you and me."

"Great," I replied.

3

Reliving the Nightmare

I am forgotten by them as though I were
dead; I have become like broken pottery.
—Psalm 31:12

At first, my lows would be that I was locked down all the
time in a 8 x 8 cell with only a 6 x 7 walk space. My head
would continually swim. I would count bars, blocks,
cracks and holes in the wall . . . Staring at three walls and
a set of bars is the most upsetting, humiliating circum-
stance anyone could ever find themselves in. To sit in a
cell is to eventually figure out the things that you can do,
and not what you can't do. When you think of the things
you can't do, incarceration becomes literally, hell.

Letter from prison by Barry Chubick, Jr.

The next Wednesday, Jim and I met outside the jail. We
discussed who should meet with Barry and who should
visit with other inmates who agree to see a chaplain. Jim
was convinced that I should see Barry again so as not to
overwhelm him. Thus, I went back to visit Barry. He
seemed glad to see me. He was still jumpy, but he wasn't
shaking as uncontrollably as he had been the previous
week. I asked him how things had gone since I had seen
him last. Barry said that it had been very difficult. "Everything," he said, "was like a nightmare. It's all a bad
dream that won't go away." The crime hounded Barry's

thoughts when he tried to sleep. He said to me slowly and methodically, "They think I did this. How could I have hurt Jane? I loved her. I would never have let anything happen to her. How can I make them understand? Why is this happening to me?"

Barry would go through a process of denial for several weeks. Each time he seemed to be in a daze as he told me how he could not have been involved in Jane's death, because he just wasn't capable of such a thing. I had seen this pattern in inmates many times in the past. There would be denial upon denial.

I listened and tried to comfort Barry with positive words about what we could do for that day, and what we could make of tomorrow. "You know, Barry," I said, "we cannot change anything about the past. We can live for today with an eye towards the future. But not even Christians can change the past." In any event, it was not the charge of Jim and me to act as Barry's judge and jury. Rather, we committed ourselves to provide him with comfort and the presence of the Holy Spirit.

In the course of my earlier jail ministry in the state of Illinois, I had several prisoners proclaim their innocence to me. After hearing their stories, I had to consider that there were at least some who might have been innocent of the crimes with which they had been charged. However, I learned early on at the Cook County Jail, that the courts didn't necessarily care if you were guilty or innocent—especially if you were poor, or African-American, or Hispanic. Several times I sat in on trials and watched as prisoners were led into the courtroom in prison garb and shackles. The judge would ask the defendants if they had had a chance to meet with their public defender. If the answer was no, as it often was, the judge would then try to reschedule a date for a new court appearance. The date would have to be agreed upon by the judge, the state's attorney and the public defender. This usually meant a delay of three or more weeks. More than once, I heard the comment made that this date, or that date, would not work because one of the court players had a golf game. Consequently, the accused, presumed innocent until proven guilty in a court of law, would go back to an overcrowded cell area to wait until their next court date. I was aware of several circumstances where people languished behind bars for several months waiting for their day in court. It gave a whole new meaning to the phrase "the right to a speedy trial."

When the public defenders could finally steal some time in their over-loaded schedule to meet with a prisoner, they would often bring the prisoner bad news. The first piece of bad news was that it didn't matter whether they were guilty or innocent. The second parcel of woe was that the public defender didn't have the time or the budget to track down leads, or witnesses. So the best course of action, according to them, was to plead guilty, serve a little time, and move on. The alternative was to be found guilty in the courtroom. If that happened, there was a good chance that the judge would crack down on the accused with a heavy sentence for having taken up their valuable court time. In case after case, I witnessed the "plea bargain" in action.

We know that the guilty plea or the claim of innocence has to come from the heart, and then only God really knows what the truth is. So Jim and I do our best to work with the Holy Spirit to provide an environment for truth to be heard. Human courts are secondary where the spiritual soul is concerned.

We knew that it was imperative that Barry got right with God. Along those lines, I was able to gently touch on some verses from the Bible. One particular section was from Paul's Letter to the Philippians at chapter 4, verses 6 and 7, where the Apostle instructs us not to worry about anything and to pray for everything. By doing this he says, we will have the divine peace of God, which is beyond human understanding. Several times over the following months, Barry and I came back to this verse for serenity.

Even though this was only our second hour together, I carefully turned our discussions to some more Bible language. Barry received this religious transition well. Somewhere in our discussions, Barry expressed a wish for a Christian songbook so he could sing a little to himself. I told Barry I would try to get him one for the next week, if I could. I asked him if it would be okay if we had a closing prayer, and we did. In that prayer, I asked God to give Barry strength and inner peace to deal with everything, one day at a time. We also prayed for the Ruby family. Barry's eyes became teary.

As I prepared to leave, Pastor Jim came over to Barry's cell. He had been counseling another prisoner in the cell area directly behind Barry's. I introduced Barry and Jim as they shook hands through the bars. I was immediately struck by the compassion of Jim's words. In a soft but firm voice, Jim told Barry we would try to be in his corner as much as possible. I continued to listen carefully and watch from the side as Jim added, "With God's help, we will all get through this." I could see that there was an instant peace between Barry and Jim. Pastor Jim's words were very empathetic and moving as he and Barry talked. It was almost as if the "adoption process" was already under way. The three us, standing in this small, dark area, overpowered the space.

It was three o'clock, and time for us to leave. As we

got outside, I immediately sucked down the fresh air. Barry had been smoking earlier, and the cigarette residue in the air made my throat close. My hatred for cigarettes and the tobacco industry increased as I struggled to clear my throat. Jim suggested a soda just might be the answer. I agreed, so we climbed into Jim's black '76 Cordoba. Our destination was McDonald's. We lamented that it might be a long time before Barry could decide at the last minute that he was going out to a fast-food restaurant. We drove away from the jail in freedom, while Barry sat in a sparse jail cell with nowhere to go.

4
Who Were They?

Let the little children come to me, and do not hinder them, for the kingdom of God belongs to such as these.

—Luke 18:16

The first time I entered a prison facility was at the Cook County Jail in Chicago, Illinois. I was beginning prison ministry for my field education studies at McCormick Theological Seminary. What I remember from that initial visit was an immense overcrowding of humanity in the cell areas. As I walked past the rows and rows of cells, the men behind the bars would press up against those bars. They would reach out so that they could feel my hands. I found out later these men, overwhelmingly African-American, just wanted to touch somebody who had come in from the outside—somebody who wasn't a part of the system.

Barry Chubick, Jr. was born on May 18, 1964, at the Greater Community Hospital in Creston. He was the oldest of four children, which included two brothers, Frank and Aaron, and a sister, Monica. His family did not stay in Iowa. They moved to Illinois when Barry was still a baby.

Barry recalled a kind of religious experience when he was about four or five years old. It occurred in the waiting

18

room of a hospital while his brother Frank was being born. Young Barry saw a large ornate Bible on a coffee table. It was the *Living Children's Bible.* He sat there flipping through the pages awestruck that this was "the word of God."

Another encounter with religion a few years later impacted him even more. He said about that incident, "When I was a child I once walked with Jesus and was enrolled in Sunday School across the street from me at a Lutheran Church in Ponca City, Oklahoma. One Sunday we each made a wood plaque. We sanded the wood to make it smooth and then varnished it to make it shine. We were then given a number of Scriptures, a box of alphabets made of pasta, and a bottle of glue. Out of the Scriptures, I chose John 3:16. I then neatly arranged and glued all the letters in sequence to the Scripture, 'For God so loved the world that he gave his one and only Son, that whoever believes in him shall not perish but have eternal life.' As I gazed in pride at the plaque I made, somehow I knew that Scripture was the most important of all!" Those words that Barry learned as a child from John 3:16, would literally become his lifeline and his existence as an adult charged with murder and assault.

Regrettably, the enthusiasm that the plaque generated for Barry was severely tempered by the pastor. One Sunday, the Chubick family missed church services. The pastor responded to their absence with a visit of his own to their house. Barry remembers sitting on the couch in the living room while the pastor berated them for not being in attendance. Then came the gripping words from the mouth of the preacher: "You will all burn in hell if you skip church!" That was the day Barry's family quit going to services, but they continued to send the children there to Sunday School.

Later, Barry and his family moved to Roseville, Illinois. It was there, in the Land of Lincoln, Barry was turned on to pot. Some of his relatives came up from Texas for a visit. Thus Barry hung out with his cousins, David, Bill, and Peggy. The Texas cousins were a bit on the wild side, and they strongly encouraged Barry to smoke some weed. He was thirteen years old at the time. In addition to their enjoyment of wacky tobacco, the Texas cousins had a fondness for fast cars.

Eventually, Barry's family moved to Coolidge, Arizona and he did not see his cousins much after that. There he met a family that befriended him and drove him back and forth to a community church, several miles outside of Coolidge. At that church, Barry was baptized by full immersion into the Christian faith.

Within a few years, Barry's lead-footed cousins met untimely deaths. In 1980, Bill was driving a car in Illinois at speeds of 100 miles per hour. He came upon a place appropriately named "Dead Man's Curve" where he hit a tree, and predictably, was killed. Just three years later, David was involved in a fatal crash with a car and a train. Still another cousin of Barry's, named Todd, crashed a car into a telephone pole and was killed. The constant specter of death around Barry caused him to be depressed and withdrawn. Thus, in an attempt to ease the pain, Barry turned to drugs and alcohol.

There were distractions in Arizona that gave Barry and his pals some fun. For instance, they would drive over to Flagstaff in a pick-up truck and fill the bed up with snow. The object was to drive back home before all the snow melted. Beer was always a part of what Barry and his friends were up to. Sometimes Barry went to the store and put a case of beer on the counter. Then he would grab the case and run out of the store without paying for it. For those occasions when they decided to pay cash for their beer, Barry and his friends would sell plasma. After selling the plasma, they would quickly drink a quart of beer and really get looped. If people donated plasma eight times per month at that particular collection center, their names would be thrown into a drawing for $100 cash. One day in 1987, Barry and his friend Mike went to give plasma, only to discover that Barry had won the prize money. They took the hundred dollars and headed for the nearest liquor store. After their purchases, Barry and Mike decided on a whim, to drive from Coolidge to El Paso, Texas. So armed with a case of beer buried in a cardboard box of ice on the back seat of their car, and with Barry behind the wheel, they hit the road.

As they were driving through Bowie, Arizona, Barry became sleepy. He remembers struggling to keep his eyes open. His next recollection was waking up just before the tremendous impact of hitting a semi-truck that was parked on the shoulder of the highway. Barry was thrown from the car. He started to come to as he lay in the middle of the road. A stranger stood over him and asked Barry if he was okay. Someone else brought a blanket and covered him. As Barry gently lifted and turned his head, he could see sparks flying through the air. He would later learn from his hospital bed in Bowie about his injuries. These included a broken hip-socket, multiple pieces of broken glass embedded in his shoulder, head and hip, and some other internal injuries. Barry was also informed that Mike had to be cut out of the car, thus accounting for the sparks he had seen.

Barry was brought in to see Mike in the ICC Unit in Tucson. Barry held Mike's hand as he lay there in a coma. Later that night, the medical staff turned off all the machinery that kept Mike alive. Eventually, Barry was charged with D.W.I. and spent sixty days in the Cochise County Jail. The prosecutor wanted to charge Barry with involuntary manslaughter, but he concluded from the skid marks of the car that Barry was not driving at excessive speeds. However, there were several other occasions that landed Barry behind bars for D.W.I. and for public intoxication.

As Barry grew out of his teen years, he lived a nomadic lifestyle by moving around Arizona, California, Florida, and Oklahoma. In the latter, Barry hooked-up with a four-time loser and burglarized a railroad car. They found a wallet there filled with credit cards. They bought a car and went on a drinking binge and credit card spending spree. Their dangerous fun ended abruptly as the long arm of the law caught up to the pair. Barry ended up spending a year in Helena, Oklahoma at a minimum-security prison.

Jane Ruby was born Jane Marie McDonnell on January 5, 1955, in Perth Amboy, New Jersey. She was the middle sibling between two brothers. She held a special fondness for dogs and enjoyed the three that she and Barry shared together. Jane paid close attention to any dog commercials or dog-related shows that would come on television. On more than one occasion, she had to bail the elusive Sam out of the dog pound.

For musical pleasure, Jane liked to listen to the Kinks and the Beatles. Barry was convinced that Jane had a mad crush on Ringo Starr. She enjoyed bowling, along with fishing and camping. Her favorite dish was anything pasta, and the sweet and sour shrimp that Barry would prepare for her. They made it a point to be together on Thanksgiving and Christmas with each other, and with Dana. Barry recalled that Jane loved her daughter Dana, and how much they enjoyed exchanging gifts at Christmas. On that holiday, Barry would garner many points for every box of chocolate-peanut Turtles he brought home to her. That was part of who Jane was—but as Barry once said, "Nobody knew Jane like I did."

Barry was twenty-nine years old when he came back to Creston in October of 1993 so he could be closer to his father. Barry's parents had since been divorced. He held a variety of jobs and was still using alcohol and drugs—especially crank.

In June 1994, Barry started working a factory job at the Trolli candy factory. He had to walk to work because he didn't have a car. He had known Jane Ruby only in passing from a couple of parties. A mutual friend of theirs suggested to Jane that she should drive by, to pick Barry up for work. After all, Barry walked to work and they were both employed at the same place. Consequently, one day, while Barry was walking to the factory, Jane pulled up in her late 70's, red-orange Chevy Blazer.

Barry and Jane would ride to work together every day, and on many of those same days, they would stop for a few beers at the Elm's Bar. Sometimes they would go over to the house that Barry was sharing with a male roommate and drink. Barry enjoyed Jane's company, but he was uncomfortable at the same time because Jane was a married woman. Still, they kept on seeing each other while they respected Jane's marital boundaries. Then came the December 17, 1994 Christmas party at the Bernings Restaurant. Barry and Jane danced together while Garth Brooks could be heard singing "The Dance" on the jukebox. Later that night, they returned to Barry's house to continue to party, but Barry's roommate was greatly opposed because Jane was married. The three of them argued for a few minutes until Barry's roommate drove Jane home.

As Jane's marriage came apart at the seams, her relationship with Barry became closer. Finally, after several months went by, Jane decided she was going to leave her husband. On the Saturday before Easter, in 1995, Jane and her husband had a big blow-out. So Jane left and went directly over to Barry's house. The next day, early on Easter morning, Jane's husband drove up on the lawn of Barry's house. Barry's roommate went out to try to calm him down, but tempers were flaring. Finally, Barry's roommate picked up a bat and Jane's husband retreated. Later that afternoon, Barry and Jane drove out to the Knotty Pine Restaurant, east of town on Highway 34, where they celebrated their "beginning" over a shrimp scampi dinner.

Barry and Jane fell deeply in love. She gave Barry the pet name "Bear" since he liked to buy her Teddy Bears for holidays and special occasions. One night "Bear" spent several hours in front of a crane machine pumping quarters into it at a bowling alley. Barry was trying to pull out every stuffed bear in the clear box of toys for Jane. In addition to the bear collection, Barry gave Jane jewelry and her favorite gift—chocolate Turtles. They made the typical local visit to the Roseman Covered Bridge and to the house that John Wayne was born in at Winterset, Iowa. For home entertainment, they would often purchase a case of beer and talk about the future, while drinking the night away in the house they rented. It was the small Cherry Street house that started out with a bed, a chair, an old television set, and some dishes. Barry and Jane also talked at work whenever they had a chance. Finally, Barry convinced Jane to transfer over to a work station closer to him so they could be around each other as much as possible. In addition to each other, they also had Jane's daughter, Dana, with them. Initially, Dana was short with Barry, but over time, they liked each other and got along fine. There were also now three dogs in the home—Butch, Sam, and Jersey, to keep them company.

Despite the affection Barry and Jane had for each other, there were problems with drugs. He became so stressed out from drugs, that one day, he walked away from his job at the Trolli factory. He stayed away from drugs for a short while, but eventually he started up again. So Barry found another job, this time at the Bunn-O-Matic coffee-maker factory. They did a drug test on him, so he was fired. Once again, Barry had to seek employment, which he found at a local hog farm. While Barry was working there, he was using crank very heavily. He would be at the farm, blown away on crank, with twelve-hundred squealing hogs. Soon Barry thought the hogs were yelling out his name. He recognized that he had become a slave to the crank, but he couldn't give it up. He began to believe that his drug use would kill him—and it almost did. One day at the hog farm, Barry's heart began to beat irregularly. He drove over to the hospital where Jane, accompanied by Barry's father, met him. Barry was sure this was the end and so he called out, "I love you Jane! I love you, Jane! I love you Jane!"

Barry did not die, and after several hours, he was released from the hospital. Both Jane and Barry's father were well aware of what had brought him to the ER in the first place. His father scolded Barry, "Whatever you're on, you better get off it quick!" Jane jumped in too, "You need help, Bear. Let me get you some help!" Barry was not interested and he gave her an emphatic, "No!"

Despite his bravado, the incident did shake Barry up a bit, but only enough to keep him off of crank for a week. Within a couple of weeks, Barry began to hear voices from the hogs saying, "You're gonna die. You're gonna die."

But Barry continued to drink and take drugs. Eventually, Barry quit working at the hog farm and the voices ceased.

After their living together for six years, Jane wanted to get married. Barry was thinking about it. For her forty-fifth birthday, on January 5, 2000, Barry gave Jane a ring. Yet, Jane was expecting an engagement ring, and Barry had only purchased a "promise" ring. Jane was extremely upset, and she told Barry, "I'm tired of telling people you're my boyfriend. It doesn't sound right. After this long, we might as well be married." One month later, Jane would be dead, and Barry would be sitting in the Union County Jail.

One year after the ring incident, Barry sent me a letter from prison that included a separate sheet of paper simply titled January 5, 2001. It was a reflection paper about Jane, on the anniversary of her birthday. In that piece, Barry wrote these words,

As I showered today through the noise and commotion of everyday prison life, I heard a familiar song that will forever ring through the depths of my heart. A song that sang through the soft rushing water on my face and penetrated through the emptiness of my soul. The song from the motion picture *Titanic*, "My Heart Will Go On," by Celine Dione. As I listened, sorrow engulfed my entire physical being, and a heart that once knew love is slowly deteriorating in remembrance of the love that passed like a warm summer breeze.

I closed my eyes to the warmth of the water that ran all around me to the thought of a happier day, and happier time. My mind drifted back to the time we watched that movie together holding each other through the drama-packed adventure.

As I looked over at her, I watched the beauty of her compassion through the tears that edged down her face.

That moment will always, always be written on my heart. I've asked for forgiveness as numerous times as there are sands in the sea. Although God has forgiven, my heart never will. . . . I really miss her.

Jane Marie Ruby would have been forty-six today.

5

Finding a Path

*Like newborn babies, crave pure spiritual
milk, so that by it you may grow up in your
salvation.*
—1 Peter 2:2

Pastor Jim spent several weeks teaching Barry what he
calls the "hand prayer" from chapter 4 verses 4–6 of Paul's
Letter to the Philippians out of the New Testament. According to Jim's teaching of this prayer, the index finger
represents "Rejoice in the Lord always." The middle finger represents "Praying about everything." The third finger says to, "Be yourself in God," while the little finger
means "and the peace of God which transcends all understanding, will guard your hearts and minds through
Christ Jesus." And finally, the thumb represents being
"continually thankful," and should touch every one of the
other four fingers. Jim built upon this with the Apostle
Paul's own prison experiences. Hoping to build up Barry's
inner strength, Jim reminded him a couple of times that
even though Paul was in prison—he never let prison get
into him.

It was February 23, 2000. It had been about a month and
a half since we started visiting the Union County Jail.
The jail staff was used to us being around, and they were
probably relieved that Barry was getting counseling. This

made their job easier, and so there was a feeling of friendliness and cooperation from all the staff.

Jim was set to meet with Barry. Neither Jim nor Barry can recall much about their first encounter, except that Jim proceeded along very delicately with what he called "social pleasantries." I gave Jim the songbook that Barry had requested. It was *The Hymnbook*[5] from 1955. Though dated, it boasts some Christian classics and can still be found in use in many Presbyterian churches in the United States. Barry was happy to have it, "Hey, excellent. I'm glad you remembered to bring it along. This will be perfect. Now I can sing some songs to myself."

When the hour passed, Jim offered to say a closing prayer. Barry was fine with that. He was beginning to see that prayer was a significant part of who Jim and I were and how we did things.

After Barry and Jim met, I conversed about how Barry seemed to be doing. We were both concerned because Barry's sleeping patterns were all out of whack. I saw this routine as commonplace in the Cook County Jail. Inmates became very nocturnal by sleeping throughout the day and staying up most of the night. It seemed like a way for them to fight against the inevitability of a new day, by staying awake in the hopes that maybe dawn would never come. Not only was this a concern for us, but it also was problematic at times. For example, Jim and I would arrive at the jail and find out who was interested in seeing a chaplain. We also had to decide which one of us would meet with Barry. Either Dorie, or Wilma, or Gayle, two of the other Union County Jail attendants, would tell us that Barry was sleeping. Then they would go and wake him up. Dorie noted that in those first weeks Barry slept all the time. At night he wrapped a towel around his head, which made it difficult for the staff to make sure

29

that he was still breathing. On two occasions, Barry said he didn't want to see us when we came to visit. He rolled over and went back to sleep. After both of those times, on the following visits, Barry would be sad that he missed us, and he seemed very disappointed with himself for being so lazy.

Pastor Jim and Barry had several good sessions together over the following months. Jim would usually sit stretched out in the hard plastic chair with metal legs right outside the bars of Barry's cell. Jim's large frame filled the narrow corridor between the bars and the wall. Jim always began his sessions with Barry by shaking hands through the bars and making small talk. As the hour progressed, they always gravitated to discussions about the Bible.

Next to the chair where Jim or I sat was a television set. This was an older, small-screen color TV that was propped up on a chair. The plug and cable wires were plugged up into the ceiling. When we visited, Barry almost always had the television set on. He turned down the sound when we were with him, but he left the picture on. There were times when I talked with Barry and his eyes wandered over to the TV. At some of those moments, I wondered whether Barry was really interested in the pastoral time. Yet Jim and I knew that we were friends to Barry for just a short time during the week, while the television was a twenty-four-hour companion if he needed it to be. His visitors were few, and his world consisted of only a few material items. So Jim and I let this interference go and never said a word about the TV being on. For a while though, the television set was a cause for concern. Early on in his incarceration, Barry watched as much court television as he could. At some of our early visits he started to tell us about the plots of those shows.

Then he compared situations from those television programs to his own predicament. "Do you think my case would go like that?" he asked.

Of course, it is unrealistic for anyone to try to compare a television program to his own situation, or to how a judge or a jury would react in his particular case. On two separate occasions, I told Barry, "Do yourself a favor and stop watching court shows altogether. They're not helping you at all. You seem to get worked up and distracted by them. It's just not in your best interest right now."

What Barry did not know was that I have a love-hate relationship with televisions in jails and prisons. I remember how the inmates on death row at the Pontiac Prison in Illinois had a pornography station available to them only on the night of an execution. It was obvious the prison wanted to sedate the condemned men from dwelling on their own impending fate. Another "abuse" of the use of television occurred at the Audy Juvenile Home in Chicago. The guards (called attendants) on the night shift would bring in VCR movies for the detainees to watch. These movies were always violent R-rated shows. Some of the viewers being held in the detention center were as young as twelve years old. These flicks were hardly the stuff of rehabilitation. These movies were used to keep the kids occupied for a couple of hours during the evening. As chaplains, we were in competition to get the kids to talk with us. Why would they talk to a "clergy man" when they could have the Terminator instead? Still, I know that TV helps inmates eat away their time. In any event, after the second time Barry and I had the discussion about watching court shows, he seemed to give them up and never mentioned them again.

One of the recollections that stood out in Barry's mind of his visits with Pastor Jim was of Jim's little black

Bible. It was a small 3 1/2 by 6-inch soft-cover *King James Version* of the Bible that an elderly couple had given to Jim a few years before. The Bible that Barry saw was well worn from use. Jim carried it in the right-front pocket of his pants. He carried it so much that it began to wear a square outline in the material. Jim would take it out while he sat with Barry. When they got along into the theological discussions, Jim would unconsciously tap that little black Bible on his knee as they talked. His tapping became almost harmonious to the talk at hand. What was particularly interesting about that Bible was the fact that it was a "misprint." The cover was upside down from the pages inside of it. Somehow, that little Bible was a large metaphor for the drama that was set before us. A short while after our time with Barry came to an end, I suggested to Pastor Jim that he send the Bible to Barry in prison. I was disappointed to learn that Jim's little black Bible was thrown away after having just about disintegrated from use.

While Barry was making noticeable progress, Jim and I also counseled other inmates. From these, we had a couple of other, of what we call "spiritual victories." In one instance, I spoke on behalf of an individual at his trial. Jim and I don't just testify for anyone who asks. Our litmus test is that there needs to be a sense of real change in the person. In this individual there was. His case was like almost every criminal case that we see in America—drug related. Southwest Iowa has been particularly vulnerable to the methamphetamine drug trade. The Iowa Division of Narcotics recently reported that the seizure of meth labs went from just eight in 1995 to 502 in 1999.[6]

The person I was going to speak for in court had been in and out of the system several times. Now, he was just ready and willing to be with his little family. Consequently, there was a definite desire to say "no" to drugs, and "yes" to God. However, for him, and for so many other drug-users and addicts, there will be an ever-present temptation to use drugs again. It's almost as if the drugs are out there waiting to swallow victims into the abyss while state after state continues to fill their jails and prisons, with drug-related offenders.

There had been another, more powerful victory. Enter David Lee Reynolds. David and I had met for only a couple of sessions, I had sensed that David had reached a certain level of spiritual peace through his own search for a personal relationship with God. At that time, in his late forties, David had had enough of the slavery of using drugs. Finally, one Wednesday, David had said he was ready to walk the talk with and for, Jesus—he was ready to be baptized. I had felt his desire to do so was honest. David and Barry were at the same stage of their Christian walk, yet they had had no contact with one another in the Union County Jail. Barry was segregated from the other inmates, mainly because of the physical configuration of the jail.

Neither Jim's church nor mine have a baptismal pool. Therefore, we planned to make a very special request to the chief jailer, Dave Danielson. We were going to ask if David could be transported to the northwest corner of town where we could administer a full-immersion baptism in the pool of the Southern Prairie YMCA. I saw David on Wednesday, April 19th of Holy Week. My mind was on all the things that had to get done for Easter. In addition, I was trying to figure out how I might get home for a few hours to celebrate my youngest daughter's first birthday. David had just found out that on the following Monday, he was going to be transferred to another facility. Thus, we would not have time to get the immersion baptism lined up. That posed another hurdle for us. Because it was Holy Week, Jim and I were booked with church duties through Easter Sunday. Finally, we decided to go back to the jail on Easter after services and baptize David by sprinkling water on him.

On that Easter Sunday, two ordained persons from my church joined Jim and me. They were Elder Cindy Edwards and her husband, Deacon Tracy Edwards. I grabbed the water bowl out of the baptismal font after service, on the way out the door of the church, and drove over to the jail. There David, Jim, Cindy, Tracy and I gathered inside the small visiting area of the jail where the two-way phones were set up for non-contact visits. Jim held the baptismal bowl as I administered the Sacrament of Baptism. There was barely enough space in the room for me to move my hand from the water in the bowl to David. As the waters of baptism were sprinkled generously over his head, "in the name of the Father, and of the Son, and of the Holy Ghost," David began to gently weep. Tears trickled down his cheeks. As the tears made their way down to his chin, they dripped off into the baptismal bowl that Jim was clutching. After administering the water, Jim sealed the moment with a prayer. Then we all shifted around so each one of us could give David a hug and a real contact visit. That was an Easter Sunday baptism that none of us will ever forget. In the most recent correspondence I have received from David, via letters from prison, he informed me that he continues in the work of the Lord.

The Holy Season was finished. The very next morning I was leaving for a vacation with my family to Atlanta to visit my brother. As is usually the case, by the time vacation came around, the demands of pastoral ministry left Jim and me exhausted. This vacation was no exception. I sat on the airplane and closed my eyes. I was totally spent. I prayed for Barry, knowing that I would not see him for a week and a half. Then I thanked God for David's baptism.

6

A Tree Starts to Grow

I planted the seed, Apollos watered it, but God made it grow. So neither he who plants nor he who waters is anything, but only God, who makes things grow.

—1 Corinthians 3:6–7

Whenever Barry had doubts about it all, he would start to lean on the criminal justice system as the great hope. Then I would tell him, "Barry, if you look for justice in the criminal justice system you will be let down. Look for justice in God. He will never let you down. Are you searching for truth in the criminal justice system? It's elusive. But our God is the God of truth. Quit seeking pain release from human institutions because they will fail you. But God will never fail you."

Afterwards, Barry would always come around and he would smile.

At the end of February, I brought him a Bible to add to his small book collection. Barry's library included the Christian songbook and a western novel that had been left in the limited jail library of hand-me-down donations. Barry began reading the Bible from the first day I brought it to him. It was a black hardcover *Revised Standard Version* that had been left over from the time when our church had purchased the *New Revised Standard Version* for the pews. Despite the small type font of that Bible, Barry began to inhale it during the day and before sleep at night. In fact, he began to read it so much that before long, he had memorized several passages as well as whole sections. Not only had Barry begun to recognize Jesus Christ as his friend, but he had also started to think theologically. We saw Barry become a disciple of Christ right before our eyes. His knowledge of Scriptures and insights had far surpassed those of many people who had been Christians for several years. It was particularly fun to spend some time with him—a person who could thoughtfully talk about the Scriptures. All three of us enjoyed that. This was one of many unexpected joys that we all encountered in our time together. Another joy was that Barry had gone well beyond our expectations for spiritual growth.

The weeks started to come, one after another. Barry was sleeping more soundly, and the denials of his involvement in Jane's death had ceased. By springtime, Barry had a great deal of head knowledge of the Bible bouncing around in his mind. He decided he needed a new outlet for it. So he developed a board game based on Bible trivia. He drew it out with a blue pen onto a piece of gray cardboard that was left over from one of his legal pads. He made up one hundred draw cards on little cut squares of notebook paper. Each one had a Bible trivia question on it. According to Barry's rules, a correct answer would advance you around the board. The goal was to get to the top of the stairway into heaven. Barry memorized all one hundred questions that he had created and their corresponding answers. It didn't take Barry long to realize that Pastor Jim had a mind like a steel trap for the location of Scriptures in the Bible. He can move across the Old Testament to the New Testament like a walking file cabinet. Jim has a disciplined ability to recall where passage after passage is, and what it says, without opening the Biblical text. One day Barry challenged Jim to play him in a game of "Barry's Bible Trivia."

I had seen these kinds of match challenges in jail before. I specifically recall a game of chess in Chicago in which one person played with his back to the table. The Cook County Jail had a kind of quirk in its system. When death row inmates had appeals on their death sentences, they were brought back from death row, and placed in the basement of Division One at the jail. There they would be able to come out of their cells during the day and spend time in a common cell area with other "dangerous" inmates. This was a luxury that few condemned inmates had on death row. I visited them once a week in that common area. The correctional officer would open the jail door for me and my colleague, Sister Miriam Wilson. We would sit in that common area with the men for about two hours. On one particular day, a death row inmate whom I had visited at the Pontiac Prison in Pontiac, Illinois, was back in Division One for an appeal. He had been playing chess with another inmate. A spirited debate broke out between them as to who really was the better chess player. The death row inmate I knew from Pontiac offered to finish the game with his back to the table and promised he would win within fifteen moves. The two opponents wagered cigarettes, as did the other inmates who gathered around us. The Pontiac inmate took one last look at the chess pieces on the board, turned around, and then began to play. Each move took on an aura of drama as it was verbally called out by a trusted third party. Sure enough, the Pontiac death row inmate won the game and the cigarettes on the fifteenth move. He never once turned around to look at the chessboard during the match. It was the most fun those inmates had had in a long time.

I was really hoping to witness a Bible trivia match between Barry and Jim. I could tell that Barry was confident, and really wanted to show us exactly how much work he had been doing. However, given our time constraints of only one-hour per week, the challenge never took place. Barry's enthusiasm over the Bible trivia game that he had created brought a big smile to his face each time we talked about it. His ingenuity did not stop there. One day he took a sock, and unraveled it. From the threads of that sock Barry made little black crosses for Jim and me. There was a proud and peaceful smile on his face the day he presented me with one. Still another time, Barry took out a piece of gray cardboard, and with a blue pen, he drew out a monopoly game solely from memory. And his rendition was a perfect replica of that famous board game. The draw cards for "Barry's Monopoly," like the draw cards for "Barry's Bible Trivia" were made on small pieces of notebook paper that were cut into squares.

Barry had been moved to the back section of his cell area so that the jail could accommodate a female prisoner with some privacy.

While Barry was in that back section, another inmate, Casey Brodsack, who was charged with complicity in a murder from a decade earlier, had been placed in the adjoining cell. Once in a while, Barry and Casey would be allowed out of their cells so they could sit in a narrow corridor that was locked down. There they played "Barry's Monopoly." At other times, Barry called out the moves from his cell to Casey's cell and then directed the players around on the board. Barry also prodded Casey to play the Bible trivia game. But Casey was no match for Barry, so his interest in playing waned. Many times in jail, and in prison, I have seen how creative the human spirit can be when a person tries to keep from being overcome by boredom. Barry was no exception.

Another creation of Barry's was a pen sketch, again on gray cardboard. This was the only real artwork that Barry had done. My experience had been that there seemed to be a large number of right-brained, artistically gifted people, who are incarcerated. People with right-brain tendencies often have artistic talents. I saw countless art pieces from the talented people in prison cells and on death row. In fact, I was so impressed by paintings I saw on death row that I took up oil painting myself. Many times, people in prison didn't realize their talents until they were inside the prison walls. One day at the Cook County Jail, a correctional officer opened a closet and discovered several paintings and drawings that inmates had done over a couple of years. All of them were on religious themes. The officer wanted them thrown away. I happened to come over to the corridor at that moment. I offered to carry all of those pieces away. I took them home and mounted each one on poster boards of varying colors. They were then used on our traveling information booth for the Kolbe House prison ministry team I was working with. What had been intended for the trash was given new life, and in turn, provided hope for others.

Jim and I knew that Barry had turned a huge corner. He was no longer lethargic or apathetic. He was sleeping in the night after his regimented Bible study and was awake during the day. We had also gotten past another topic that was getting Barry down quite a bit. It had to do with his personal possessions on the outside. He told me that a person he thought was his friend had gone into his apartment and stolen all of his worldly possessions. This information came from third-party friends. Barry said in a harsh tone to me, "They stole my TV, stereo, and anything else of value that I had. Look, I'm in here and now everything I owned is taken. Jane's gone. I have nothing. The police aren't interested in trying to get any of my stuff back either."

When Barry was upset about this, I reminded him that he was in the process of making a new start with his person and his life. "Barry, I know you feel very cheated by all of this," I said. "But really, we shouldn't be mad at this guy who took your stuff. We need to pray for him because obviously he doesn't know Jesus. And anyway, you don't need those material things right now."

"Yeah, I know it," Barry answered. Again he said, "It's just that everything in the world is being taken away from me. Jane is gone . . . all my stuff . . . our dogs."

Invariably we would take time out to pray for the thief, and after a few weeks, Barry was at peace with the loss of his material world back at his house. Barry did understand that he was becoming a different person, and that his new life was going to center around God. If God didn't think he needed those material possessions, so be it.

The Bible stories that Barry read every day and into the night were making sense to him. We knew in our heart of hearts that God was revealing Himself to Barry through the Word. As we watched this transformation in progress, Jim and I could not help but wonder out loud how things might have been different if we had met Barry before the murder. Would he have been able to grasp the mysteries of God and the saving power of Jesus Christ? After all, there were seeds of religion in Barry's childhood. Maybe the tragedy could have been avoided. As we considered these possibilities, we did so, fully aware that there are many more people around us who desperately need intervention—but how to reach them?

At one of our Wednesday meetings, I reminded Barry what Jesus said in Luke 12:48b: "From everyone who has been given much, much will be demanded; . . ." Therefore since he was in tune with the ways of God, he had a responsibility to share the Good News. I asked Barry if he had been trying to teach any of the jail staff about the Good News. Barry said, "Sometimes when Dorie is working the night shift, she will come in to check on me. I will say something funny to her in order to try and get a conversation going. Then I always make a connection back to the Bible." Barry had a coy smile on his face when he told me this. I could tell that he enjoyed the friendly banter and the challenge of planting Godly seeds around Dorie.

Jim and I knew that Barry was changing dramatically as a person. We were also aware that he was carrying a heavy burden. Thus, we knew that over time, Barry's new walk with Jesus Christ would be tested decisively.

7

Unchangeable Moments

I am the gate; whoever enters through me will be saved.

—John 10:9

The sorceries are blinding the truth. All things will be revealed to he who seeks the truth. Nothing will be left covered. When you see the truth you will recognize it. He will come like a thief in the night. Those found in sorcery will be left behind. I will turn my back, they will be devoured by the enemy. Hear my warning because the time is near, even at the door. Repent and seek me and I will accept you into the Kingdom. ... The sorceries are blinding the truth. The truth about methamphetamine is that it is the purest form of sorcery on earth today. The biggest most subtle lie of Satan today is that meth is just another drug. (Steven Box).[7]

Through conversations with Barry, and with letters from prison from him, I have constructed the following chain of events that Barry must live with for the rest of his life. The story began to unfold on Saturday, February 5, 2000. Barry and Jane had been invited to a birthday party on that date by a close friend of Jane's named Sylvia.[8] This gig was to be a surprise birthday party for Sylvia's husband, Bob, and was to be held at a local bowling alley.

Jane went over early that afternoon to help Sylvia set up for the party.

Barry stayed home and slept in late. After he finally pulled himself out of bed, Barry lay around and watched television. He was very restless that day. Eventually, he started to get the urge for some meth. It didn't take very long before the urge turned into a craving. So Barry left his house and drove the ten miles over to Afton, to the house of a friend named Bill, where Barry thought he could score some drugs. Bill's brother Jake was there when Barry arrived. Bill asked if he could borrow Barry's cell phone, which had been a Christmas present from Jane. They made several calls in the hopes of making a drug buy. The effort was futile, though, they couldn't flush any out. So they began to drink beer and watch television.

As they just hung out together, Barry told Bill that Jane was busy helping Sylvia get ready for Bob's surprise birthday party. They continued to make calls on the cell phone, but they were still unable to reach any of their contacts. Again Barry was feeling restless, so he decided to leave Bill's house. He drove back to Creston. Along the way, he stopped at a Casey's gas station to buy some beer. Then Barry went back home and took a shower. He put on a suit coat and jeans for the party. He continued to drink beer. Barry dialed the bowling alley on his cell phone to tell Jane that he was ready for the party. Jane left the party preparations in her Blazer, and picked up Barry. Jane told him, "You look good, Bear."

"Thank you, Jane," he told her. Then they hugged each other and kissed.

Barry told Jane that he had brought along a deck of cards for the party. He liked to do card tricks, and he thought maybe it would liven things up at the party in case it turned out to be a yawner. When they arrived at the party, Barry could see that there was plenty of food to eat. That didn't really matter to Barry, however, since he never ate much when he was drinking. After a while of mingling and drinking, Barry sat down at a table with Sylvia and Bob and began to do some card tricks. By now, Barry was "feeling good" from the alcohol that he had consumed. He was also enjoying the attention of being the "card master." Barry started out with a "very clever card trick" called Red and the Bartender, which uses the full deck. Everyone at the table was amazed at the sleight of hand, and they told Barry he had to show some other people what he could do with those cards. So Barry went around to various tables, showing them the card trick. At one of the tables, he started drinking what he remembers as "some kind of liquor concoction" from a pitcher. This complemented the massive quantities of beer that he had already drunk.

Yet another time, Barry felt restless. He decided on a whim to go home and change into some clothes that were more comfortable. On the short drive home, Barry was still craving some meth, and, he was thinking about where he might be able to find some. Impulsively, Barry returned to the party where he took a seat at a table with Jane and Sylvia. By this time, the keg was empty. Everyone reached into his or her pockets in order to buy another one so the drinking could continue. Meanwhile, Barry and Jane decided to shoot some pool together, so they left the table and selected some pool cues. After a while, they drifted around the party again until Jane came over to Barry and told him she wanted to go dancing at the Twilight Zone, a bar across town. Barry, Jane, and Sylvia got into the car, even though all three of them were very drunk. They decided that Barry was in the best shape of the three, so he was designated as the driver.

At the Twilight Zone, Barry and Sylvia hit the dance floor together while Jane danced with someone else. As they were jammin' away, Barry saw a woman who had been able to supply him with meth in the past. Despite his level of intoxication, Barry still had a yearning for some meth. He was able to buy a quarter ounce from her. Barry went into the restroom to take it.

The events that took place after Barry went off to do meth are difficult for him to remember. For instance, Barry knows that he and Jane drove Sylvia home later on, but he can't recall dropping her off. Back at home, Jane went to bed, but Barry was in no mood to sleep. Instead, he pulled out mixed drinks from behind his home-bar set. The bar, stools, light, stereo and liquor cabinet were all part of Christmas presents from Jane a few years earlier. Barry cannot remember how many mixed drinks he made and drank, except that there were many. The more alcohol Barry consumed in the early morning hours of what was now the 6th of February, the more lonesome he became for his family in Arizona. His loneliness finally became too much, so he placed a call to his brother Aaron. He told Aaron how much he missed him and Frank and their mother. They talked at length until Jane yelled at Barry to get off the phone. For reasons Barry really never understood, Jane would get upset anytime he called home. Barry was kind of used to her quirk about these calls, so he tried to end the conversation with Aaron. But Jane was clearly getting very angry. She yelled at Barry again, "You're out of the house tomorrow! Get off the phone!" Barry said good-bye to Aaron and hung up the phone.

A short time later, the phone rang, and Jane answered it. "It's for you. It's your brother," she mockingly told Barry. It was Aaron calling back. Jane in turn, stomped out of the house. "See what I have to put up with . . ." Barry wearily confided to Aaron. A depressed and drug-induced Barry then gave his brother a scare: "I'm just going to take a knife and fall on it."

"No, Barry, no! Don't do anything like that!" was Aaron's terse reply.

Aaron continued to talk Barry out of his sadness. Barry did begin to feel better for a short while. But after he finished the call and hung up, Barry could feel the blackness of depression taking over once again. In his anguished state Barry agonized over his drug habit, which he believed was ruining his life and driving a wedge between himself and Jane. Barry's depression started to spiral down—fast. He went down into the basement and rummaged around for an aerosol can. He found one that he used to make model cars with. Then Barry took a clean sock out of the dryer and sprayed paint on one side of it. He folded the sock over his face and began to take long and fast breaths. Barry considered that he had a friend who had once died from doing the same thing, but he really didn't much care about it. Barry went back upstairs and sat at the bar. Once again he wrapped the sock around his face and breathed in hard. He was hoping to pass out, and maybe even never wake up. Barry estimated the time as somewhere around 3:00 A.M., although he wasn't really sure.

Sometime after that, Jane and Barry had another fight. According to the police report, Barry grabbed Jane by the neck and choked her. Jane left the house and went over to her daughter Dana's house. Jane told Dana that she wanted to go back home to get some things. She convinced Dana to go with her. When they returned, they found Barry on the couch in the living room. They noticed that Jersey the dog, was tangled up under the couch. This might have set Barry off. Dana heard her mom screaming, "He's got a knife! Get out of the house! He stabbed me! Get out of the house!" As Jane ran from the house, Dana confronted Barry. He then took a swipe at her with the knife, hitting her in the side. As Barry recoiled with the knife, Dana grabbed it with her hand and they struggled.

Barry's next memory had him on the couch with people screaming at him. He was on top of Dana, and he was wielding some kind of kitchen knife. Suddenly, Barry felt a crushing blow to his head that sounded to him like breaking glass. He looked down, and a thought of terror ran through his mind, "Oh, God, what am I doing! Oh, God, what have I done!" Dana was able to get out of the house and over to her mom's car. Jane was in the passenger seat moaning. Dana knew she had to get her mom to the hospital as soon as possible, so they raced off in that direction.

Barry does not remember having stabbed anyone. The next sensation that overtook him was that of a great weight—not the weight of another human being—but the weight of the moment. He dropped to his knees in shock. All the while, his mind was bouncing around, "What have I done? What am I going to do?"

In an instant, Barry jumped up and ran. He got into his car, a 1976 white-oven brown Mercury. (Apparently, both Jim and Barry have an affinity for Bicentennial-era automobiles.) Barry sped off into the freezing Iowa winter night. It wasn't until Barry was driving east on Highway 34 that he realized he wasn't wearing shoes or socks. He also didn't have a coat. He drove only half conscious of the physical surroundings speeding past him. The questions that continued to rush through his head consumed him. "Why has this happened? Where is Jane stabbed at? Oh, God, what if she dies? Where did you stab her? In the stomach?"

Barry drove back over to Bill's house. He fell to the ground on his hands and knees and cried out, "Help me please! Somebody help me."

Bill came out and asked Barry, "What happened?"

He answered him, "I stabbed Jane." As he said this, Barry was crying uncontrollably and still asking for help.

Barry wasn't sure Bill believed him, so he just blurted out, "Jane's dead!"

"Where is she?" Bill wanted to know. "Is Jane at home?"

"No. Do you have any shoes and socks?" Barry wanted to know. His feet were frozen.

8

Backsliding and Despair

*Even though I walk through the valley of the
shadow of death, I will fear no evil, for you
are with me.*

—Psalm 23:4

It's another Wednesday afternoon. Barry is very distracted. Finally he says, "I saw on the news that some
woman shot another woman to death in a road rage thing.
They said she is gonna get manslaughter. Now how can I
be lookin' at fifty years for my crime when I was under the
influence at the time? It doesn't seem fair. It just doesn't
seem right. How can this be the case?"

I hear his frustration and fear as I try to respond, "Ya
know, I really can't answer that, Barry, except to say that
fairness is very often not a part of the hurricane we call
criminal justice in this country. That's just how it is."

Barry stares down at the floor in disgust with his feet
in orange slippers dangling back and forth.

I was usually pumped up to go see Barry. My wife noted
that I always got a natural high when I went in to do jail
ministry. She said it seemed as if jails and prisons would
be such dreary places. But, I did get excited to go behind
bars. However, it took an extra effort to get motivated to
go in to this jail during the Iowa summer of 2000, which
was particularly hot. That meant the Union County Jail

was even hotter. The jail cells are located on the second floor in a building where the air conditioning doesn't work and there are no windows. Barry would spend many of those sweltering summer days in his bare chest because of the heat. As we talked, I usually slumped back on the hard plastic chair with my legs extended and my feet up against the bars. Barry sat on his bed. Sweat literally poured out of both of us. We must have been a sad sight for the small camera mounted on the ceiling watching our every move. The heat made it a struggle to be a good listener. Yet Barry's enthusiasm to have Jim and me there made up for the misery.

On those very hot days, the female jail attendants sometimes wore shorts and t-shirts. I wondered if Barry had difficulty being locked up while he watched the women walking around in shorts when they came back to his area. Barry said it wasn't a problem. Later on, I asked Dorie if she ever felt that Barry had been leering at her, and she said she had never felt he was.

There were other challenges to deal with. At some of our visits, Barry was very sad because he missed Jane so terribly. There were periods when he would weep for her for fifteen minutes or so. These were painful moments for all of us. Dorie also remembers that for several days after Barry was arrested, he sat on the floor in the shower and wept, presumably for Jane.

Once I asked Barry to describe an especially difficult time in jail. His response was wrapped up in his loss of Jane, "When the first nice day came, they opened the back door of the jail to let some fresh air in. I got off my bunk and stood at the bars. As I grabbed the bars trying to look outside to see any kind of daylight or life or movement, I heard some birds chirping away so beautiful. I thought of Jane, and tears rolled down my face as I thought she would never hear that again. I hurt so bad that day as I continued listening to those birds."

Then came the most challenging event for all of us to deal with. It happened on Thursday, June 8, 2000. Dorie had told me that sometimes at night, Barry would toss things out of his cell if he wasn't in a particularly good mood. I had seen this many times in prison ministry as a way for an inmate to let off steam, or to protest a prison edict, like a lockdown. On this night, though, all the pressure and the impact of Barry's alleged crime came crashing down on him. On Friday afternoon I received a call from Dorie at the jail. She said, "Chubick went a little bit crazy last night. He threw absolutely everything out of his cell. He was very depressed."

She said he didn't want to talk to anybody. Finally, he told Dorie that he wanted to talk to Pastor Jim. Dorie had tried to reach Jim but couldn't. I told her I would see if I could locate him for her. I knew that Jim liked to sneak off into the "wilderness" on Fridays in order to spend some quality prayer time with the Lord. Sometimes though, I could catch him coming out of the church or his house. This was not to be on that day. I could not find Jim. I called Dorie back and offered to come over. We both started laughing over the phone because this was the second time Barry had had a bad night and asked for Pastor Jim to make a special visit to talk with him. Dorie had not been able to get in touch with Jim back when this had happened before. At that I time I dropped everything and went. We found it comical that Barry would ask for Jim and get me instead. Through that light moment, I told Dorie on the phone, "Well, he doesn't get the old war-horse. So once again he'll just have to settle for second best." Dorie laughed about it on the other end.

I told Dorie that I would try to get there in about an

hour or so. I didn't want to come right over, because I didn't want Barry to think he could snap his fingers and get ministerial coverage at his beck and call, even though I was concerned about him. And the concern was warranted because Dorie said this had been a much harsher episode than the previous one. I hung up the phone and looked at my desk. Friday was supposed to be my day off. It was the day when my friend, Little Tommy D., and I, tried to go fishing in his bass boat, but there I was, like so many other Fridays, in the office trying to keep up. Now, I was going to have to walk away from my guilt stacks anyway. On the short drive over to the jail, I decided that it didn't really matter whether Barry preferred Jim's counseling to mine. Jim and I were not in competition with each other at all. Rather, we were both trying to provide pastoral care, and to plant and water some seeds of religion along the way. Whatever way it worked out was fine with both of us. However, it was that phone call with Dorie that later threw me completely off guard, as events unfolded in the courtroom at Barry's sentencing.

I got over to the jail and couldn't help but notice that the sky was very gray and ominous. I knocked on the jail door and peered into the small window that has wire mesh crossing through the glass. I heard someone coming to the door. I could always tell when it was Dorie just by the way the keys jingled in her hands. Each of the jail staff had a specific jingle with the keys, unknowingly, I was sure. As the door opened, Dorie greeted me, "Hi, Terry. I'm glad you could get here."

"Yeah, I left a mess back in my office, but . . . oh, well. Is everything still the same?" I asked.

"Still quiet back there," said Dorie. "I know Chubick will be glad you're here."

Once inside, Dorie led me back over to Barry's cell.

Barry looked very distraught. He immediately started to apologize to me for asking for Jim. "I just didn't want to be bothering you all the time," he said.

"Forget about it," I told him. "I'm here to help if possible, and that's what we need to focus on."

Barry confessed something that had him very worried. In addition to tossing everything out of his cell the previous night, he had also thrown out the Bible that I had given him. First he had torn pages out of it in a rage at God. When the pages were gone, the empty spine went through the bars. Barry was ashamed as he retold how the gift, which he had held so precious from me, had ended up in the trash. "Brother Barry," I said, "We got extra Bibles stacked up back at the church. I'll try to get you another one. In fact, I'll try to get a different version. Maybe something with a larger print size. I know what you're up against here. This kind of stuff can happen. Don't worry about it at all."

I could see a great burden was lifted from his shoulders, and a bit of a smile came back to his face. Barry felt as if he had let down a friend in a big way, and he wanted to make it right. He stood up straighter and seemed to get comfortable. I knew we were going to have a good session together.

Later, Barry recalled what went on during that night when he "just lost it." He said, "I became so depressed over Jane's death. I wanted to know why God would let this happen to me. I just wanted to give up. I sat in my cell and just cried and blamed it all on God. I even cursed Him for letting this happen to me. I gave up on everything, and ripped all my legal papers and notes up and threw them in the trash. I just couldn't believe this was happening to me. These things happen to other people, not to me. I refused seeing anyone, even my own Dad whom I love so dearly. I just wanted to die. Then I took the Bible that you gave me and threw it, and blamed God for it all. I gave up on God because I felt like He wasn't helping me—especially through all the prayers when I spoke to Him from the depths of my heart. I prayed and prayed for him to bring Jane back, not just for me, but for the family. I would rather deal with the time of fifty years than with the death of the one I loved so much. I couldn't take it anymore, and I got up and picked up the Bible and just started tearing all the pages out—handfuls at a time, until there wasn't anything left. I then took all the letters that everybody had written me and all the cards they sent me, and I threw them right through the bars. I gave up on life and everybody. All the addresses of all my family, their cards of love, all my legal paperwork, and the living Word of God, that comforted me, that I even slept with at nights and cuddled next to, were gone. Everything was gone, pieces, just like my life. After I realized everything that I tore up, I wept bitterly. I hurt then more than anything else did in the world. I brought myself to the lowest point of my life, and it's nobody's fault but mine. It was so hot in that cell that summer that I turned the shower on and stepped in, clothes and all. My heart felt as though it had been stopped. It felt like a blade piercing my heart. I just wanted God to let me die!"

Barry spent a long time in the shower. It was raised a foot off the floor, and measured only two-and-one-half-feet wide. It was seven feet high. It was there that Barry began to call out, "I'm sorry, God. I'm sorry! Please forgive me! Forgive me, God! I never meant for this to happen! I'm sorry please, please forgive me." Then Barry added, "I still remember all the words I spoke to God as the tears came down like rain."

His comment on his tears reminded me of another inmate who had struggled to try to develop a relationship with Jesus Christ. He said that one night while he was sitting in his cell he gripped a Bible in his hands. He looked up toward the heavens in anguish, and he prayed. As he prayed, teardrops fell from his eyes and landed on his Bible. He recalled that after three days those tears that fell on the Bible did not dry up. He said, "They never dried up. I finally just brushed 'em away. Now how could that be?"

Physically, Barry could not run away, but inside his person, he was trying to escape. It was as if it was the morning of February 6, 2000 again, when Barry was on his knees. His friend Bill had given him shoes and socks, but Barry wanted more. He wanted someone to really talk to—someone who would listen.

"I'm leaving! I'm running away!" Barry yelled at Bill that morning. Barry sped off in his car back out onto Highway 34 headed east. His mind was racing, "Please, somebody, stop this pain. Make everything all right."

His next thought was that he needed gas. A quick check of his wallet showed he had eight dollars to his name. Eventually he got gas, but Barry doesn't remember where or when. After he'd driven for a long time, Barry realized he was in Illinois. In a desperate attempt to make the last twenty- four hours disappear, Barry drove over to Roseville, Illinois. He thought that by going back to the place where he grew up he could "wake up" from the dream that had become a nightmare. Barry decided he needed to find out how Jane was doing. He checked his wallet again. This time it was empty, except for a calling card. He tried a couple of different numbers, but was unable to reach anyone. He decided it was time to go back to Creston to see Jane for himself. Money was a problem. He tried selling some tools from the trunk of his car. All he was able to sell was an air compressor to a guy in a bar in Monmouth, Illinois for five dollars. Then Barry pulled into a gas station and filled the tank. He drove off without paying. To help dull the pain of it all, Barry used the five dollars to buy beer at another location. By this time, Barry was exhausted as well as confused. Consequently, he drove off of the road several times and barely stayed awake behind the wheel.

Barry's story was both riveting and sad. He and I spoke for two hours on that dark Friday. The jail shift change took place on schedule, but the staff let me stay back there because they all knew Barry was hurting. I tried to reassure Barry that Christians have been known to backslide in their faith. Yet, the beauty of it is that if we tell God we are sorry in the name of Jesus Christ, then we are forgiven in that same name. Barry began to loosen up, and, by the time I left, I really felt that he was tapping into the inner peace that we both knew he had. Finally, Barry said, "You know, the weird thing about this is that even though I threw all those cards away, I got more in the mail today. There are still some people who care about me . . . love me." Then Barry started to weep as we prayed together. When I left the jail, I was physically and emotionally drained, but I had to head back to my office because the workload was still piled high on my desk.

Barry was fine after all that. The following week I brought him a *Good News Bible*.[9] It was a larger print version and an easier translation than the *Revised Standard Version* that Barry had torn up. Within one year after I gave him that second Bible, Barry shared it with several of his family members. Neither of us could have ever imagined how that replacement Bible would become such a singular tool for evangelism. It was just another example of how God will take a bad situation and use it for the good.

9

Let's Go Fly a Kite

Be patient, then, brothers, until the Lord's coming. See how the farmer waits for the land to yield its valuable crop and how patient he is for the autumn and spring rains.
—James 5:7

Jim and I discovered that along with our common interests in jail ministry and fishing we both also share a fondness for classic cars. We especially enjoy the era of the muscle cars. So when Jim finally purchased his dream machine—a red 1969 Dodge Charger with a black vinyl roof and a 440 horsepower engine under the hood, we immediately went for a ride. As we headed east on Highway 34, Jim "got on it" a bit. The weather was calm and clear while his new "baby" hauled down the road. All the windows were rolled down allowing the warm wind to blow through the interior of the car and through our hair. As I held on tightly, I couldn't help but think that this rush was the total antithesis of prison life. We were free and independent, while Barry was locked in a small cell with no place to go. Consequently, we debated about not telling Barry about the car, and the drive, so as not to hurt him with the pain of being unable to experience the ride with us. In the end, we decided we would share it with him so that he could stay connected with the outside world. As it turned out, Barry really enjoyed hearing about the retelling of the adventure.

Barry started out his incarceration very concerned about the mechanics of his case. In jails and prisons I had often heard inmates talk about their "case." It became their focus for living. Many inmates did legal research for their particular cases even though many of them could barely read or write. Sometimes, they did it so they could file an appeal. Sometimes they did it to assist their attorney when the attorney was over-worked. The latter often happened when their attorney was an overworked and underpaid public defender. Barry had two court-appointed lawyers whom he was determined to help with his case if he could. So for the first several weeks Barry always had pads of legal papers on his bed. He would go through legal documents from the courts and make voluminous penciled notes from them onto legal pads. All of the words that he had written went across the margins so as to maximize the space of the paper. At the beginning of our sessions, Barry would talk about this piece or that piece of his case. Each time there were multiple pages filled with his writings in pencil to back up his claim. "My attorneys are just not doing anything for me," he would say.

"When was the last time you spoke with them?" I would ask.

Barry gave me the same answer that I heard so many times from other people locked up in jails and prisons, "I can't get in touch with them, and they won't return my calls."

It always seemed to Barry that his legal-eagles should have been doing something for his case. Barry was very frustrated with the whole process. However, as the weeks went by, Barry did less and less legal work, until he really wasn't doing it at all.

Barry was still filling those legal pads with writings in pencil, but instead of taking notes on the mundane and dense legalese paperwork, he began to make notes on the various Biblical stories that he read. His library increased with *The Inspirational Study Bible,* by Max Lucado,[10] on which he also took notes. His cousins Roxanne, Michelle, and Tammy, who regularly visited him later in the afternoon on Wednesdays, gave this to him. Barry loved their visits and referred to his cousins as "my guardian angels." Before too long, there were stacks of legal pads filled with notes, about the Bible written in pencil. This in-depth manner of study contributed greatly to Barry's massive Biblical retention.

Barry needed another outlet for all that head knowledge he was inhaling, so he went a step further. He began to write sermons. These sermons were religious thoughts, ideas, and understandings of the Biblical texts, which were unfolding before him. His new understanding brought the truest joy that comes with the Holy Scriptures—the desire to share them with others. So as Barry wrote these 'sermons,' he sent some to Jim and me during the week. In one of those homiletics, Barry wrote, *"As Christians, we need to focus each and every day of our lives on walking in the light of Jesus Christ. Walking in His light is meditating on His Word and exercising His characteristics before others. Then the light of Jesus Christ will always sustain us."*

We would read these with interest, and also with a sense of awe, because we knew that Barry was growing in the mysteries of God. These same mysteries that he had heard and seen in his life, but didn't understand before, were now coming together in such a way that he wanted to spread the Good News with others.

Barry decided that the best way to share God's Word

was to "fly some kites" to some churches— so that's what he did. Barry began to gather church addresses from the phone directories so that he could send letters to area churches. He expanded his missive mission field to tele-vangelists. After all, Barry was watching them on televi-sion, on Sunday mornings. They were preaching to him, and he was listening. Barry wanted them to know some-one out there was hearing the message. In addition, he would do a little sermonizing of his own.

Barry often read portions of these letters to Jim and me before he sent them off. Prisoners may feel compelled to write to churches that they don't know. Almost without fail their letters solicit money. This was not the case with Barry. He just wanted to write letters so that he could share his joy in the Gospel, and expound on some story or theological point. For all the letters Barry sent out, he re-ceived only a few replies. One came from Jesse Duplantis of Jesse Duplantis Ministries.[11] He sent Barry a lengthy and compassionate letter that began: *"Thank you for sharing your situation with me. I want you to know that my staff and I have been praying for you since we received your letter."* Duplantis continued, *"Although the circum-stances may seem impossible, remember . . . you serve a God who is able to handle the impossible! All you have to do to make sure your prayers aren't hindered in repenting of any sin and release anyone you're holding unforgive-ness towards."*

Several relevant Scripture citations followed. I know Barry was pained that people were not responding to the letters that he sent out. However, that letter from Jesse Duplantis made up for them all. I can still see the big smile on Barry's face when he told me about it. "Hey, guess what?" he said, "I got a letter back from a church. Look!" Then he read the entire contents of the letter out loud to me. It strengthened his resolve to keep on writing more letters, to more churches. His enthusiasm carried on with Dorie when he told her that he had received a reply from a church.

A local letter was sent to the Crest Baptist Church. It arrived on a Wednesday when Jim and I both had to be out of town. It just so happened that we had asked the pastor of that church, Chuck Spindler, to go over to the jail for us. Pastor Chuck went over to the Union County Jail at 2:00 P.M. and met Barry. This was a surprise and a joy for Barry when he realized the letter that he sent to Crest Baptist was being answered in person, on the same day!

And then there was the letter that was returned from another Creston church. The envelope that the letter was in had obviously been opened and taped back shut. The outside of the envelope was stamped four times as, "UNDELIVERABLE AS ADDRESSED UNABLE TO FORWARD." I found this odd because the address was correct on the envelope. Here is a portion of what Barry wrote to that church,

I pray for your prosperity in faith, in kindness, in love for one another, and most of all for your love for Jesus Christ. Whose love takes us to our innermost depths that can never be humanly imagined.

Then Barry went on to write:

I would like to share something with you that touched me deeply. I ran across a prayer a few days ago. It was a prayer about the Bible. In this prayer I found something that chipped away in my heart, as I read, "Bless those who transport your Word to far-off places, to people who have not been able to open your Word." As I read this I thought, who? Who . . . hasn't opened your Word? As sorrow welled in my heart, tears rolled down my cheek, as far as I thought of those people right now, who are lonely and lost, just as I was. I couldn't imagine never having the experience of knowing Jesus Christ, our Lord and Savior.

Barry closes the letter with a request—not for money, but for prayers.

The letter was postmarked right about the time our town of Creston was celebrating the Fourth of July with its annual parade. In keeping with the season, it was very hot on parade day. I sat with my family along the parade route in front of the Ford dealership. We almost baked in the heat as we watched the floats and popular farm equipment roll by. As the celebration went on, a small group of people came along handing out religious tracts. Inside their pamphlet it said: *"Jesus Christ has made it possible for you to know for sure that if you died tonight, you would go to heaven. If you are not sure, we want to help you."* This tract came from the same church that Barry had sent the above letter to.

In these letters that Barry would send, the contents were always the same. First, he would pray for the recipient. Then he moved into a religious dissertation, usually a couple of pages in length. He closed with a promise to pray for the recipient later. In a letter that he sent to me at the First Presbyterian Church dated August 3, 2000, Barry offered this prayer: *"May your loving church prosper with all the glorious gifts and blessings that God has to offer you through your faith in our Lord and Savior Jesus Christ."*

And then one day Barry really hit a home run. It was one of those Wednesdays when Jim and I both sat with Barry. Jim was draped over his chair, while I sat back in mine with my feet up on the cell bars. Barry sat on his bed and began to talk about some ideas he had for future letters. One idea was a powerful message about the Apostle Paul.

In chapter 9 of the Acts of the Apostles, we read about Paul's dramatic conversion on the road to Damascus. According to the Biblical story, he fell to the ground while a light from heaven flashed around him. While Paul, who had been known as Saul, was lying on the ground, he heard the voice of Jesus himself. Then for the next three days, Saul was blind. As Saul sat there unable to see, the Lord sent a disciple named Ananias directly to him. There, Ananias placed his hands on Saul, and we are told that his sight was restored as "something like scales fell from Saul's eyes. . . ."[12]

As Barry recounted this story with great excitement, he told Jim and me that he had been pondering what Saul must have been going through during those three days of blindness. Barry said, "I am convinced that because Saul had these fish scales on his eyes so thick, he couldn't see anything. In fact, the only direction he could see was inside himself. And he didn't like what he saw. As Christians, I believe we were also once in the darkness, but it took the darkness to discover the true light." Then Barry quoted Psalm 119:105: "Your word is a lamp to my feet and a light for my path." After a few moments of silence, Barry put it all together: "Paul was a great author and blessing for Christianity. He was also in darkness before he saw the true light. Paul was never the same after that—but then, neither was the world!"

Jim and I looked intently at each other after hearing this. We didn't say anything, but we spoke to each other loud and clear—we knew Barry was becoming deeply in tune with the ways of God. A Biblical story about blindness recalled in a dimly lit jail gave us some keen insight into an emerging child of God. Barry was seeing and hearing more clearly in the spiritual world.

There was one other kite that Barry sent. It was addressed to the immediate family of Jane Ruby. This letter asked for forgiveness, and it contained a promise to pray for their family every day. After he read the first draft to Jim and me, we all just sat and didn't say anything for several minutes. The letter was mailed. In the end, Barry did not receive a response to it, although he really wasn't expecting to. We were proud of Barry's courage and saw this particular letter as a sign of his grasp of the need for forgiveness in our lives.

10

Tough Love

In this you greatly rejoice, though now for a little while you may have had to suffer grief in all kind of trials.

—1 Peter 1:6

You remember that *Good News Bible* you gave me? Well, when I read it, I signed it and dated it. I then gave it to my dad to read. And now he has read it and also has signed it and dated it. Now my dad has passed it on to my other brother. Dad has already bought two copies of the same *Good News Bible* and gave one to my sister here in Iowa and another to my other brother in Arizona. Now my mom is coming around. She reads all the Bible tracts I send her. My dad gave his life to the Lord, and it's changed him considerably. Now he says he hungers for more just as I did, and still do. All because of that one Bible you gave me that has touched all of my families' lives and who knows who else? I thank you very much for the chain reaction you started, but most of all I thank Jesus Christ for what he has done for me and my family.

(Letter from prison by Barry Chubick, Jr.)

At the Cook County Jail, I counseled a man who was trying—once and for all—to leave gang life, and the powerful influence it held over him. I will call him Charlie. Charlie was prepared to say "yes" to Christ and "no" to the gangs.

On the surface this might have sounded like a noble gesture, but in reality, it was even more than that. We both knew all too well that before someone could leave the gang, there had to be a punishment phase. He was told that if he wanted out of the gang, his fingers would have to be smashed in one of the cell doors. This man was ready. Charlie was committed to Christ and was prepared to bear any burden. Finally, one day he told me it was time to make the "break" as it were. "Do you want me to try to get you some protection?" I asked.

"Nope. I gotta do this thing on my own. This way God will know it's real," Charlie answered. With that he left the chaplain's office and went back down to his cell area. I did not hear any commotion as I prayed for his safety. A few days later I saw him being led away with some other inmates. He smiled across the stark corridor and yelled over to me, "Hey Pastor Terry! I did it! I told the gang chief I was quitting. And they didn't hurt me after all."

Charlie had a liberating smile on his face as he said that. In an instant, his group went around a corner and trudged down another long corridor. He got shipped on into the prison system soon after. I did receive a note from him written on a social worker request form. Charlie wrote that he had told the gang leader, and other gang members gathered around him, that he was turning his life over to Christ. They were so amazed at his boldness that they just turned and walked away. I never heard from Charlie again.

Back in Creston, Iowa, it was getting to be late September. Barry had been scheduled to go to court in August, but a delay from the courts put it off until November. Still, Jim and I knew our time with Barry was quickly slipping away. Just as the courageous Charlie stood up to the gangs and had had to make it on his own,

Barry would have to do the same in an Iowa prison. Even though Barry was cooped up in a small, dark, hot cell in Creston, we knew he was safe. Prison life is another matter, altogether.

At these last several visits, Barry and I talked about being a Christian in a prison setting. A spiritual person can feel the spiritual battleground that exists every day in prison. You can literally feel the forces of good and evil pushing each other inside the foreboding prison walls. One of the significant weapons that evil uses in prison is the gang system. Gangs are relentless on their prey and are a dominant force inside the prison setting. When a new inmate arrives at a facility, it's not too long before a gang member representative approaches him. The would-be recruit is asked to whom he belongs. The inmate might make a choice at that moment. Another possibility is that the inmate can say is that he is "into the Word." This claim would identify him as being a Christian. In some facilities, this response may cause the gangs to back off. If the gangs do give the new inmate space, they will keep a close eye on him. If the gang leadership decides he isn't living "like a Christian should," they will pay him another visit. The irony is that gangs have systematically taken Christian symbols and beliefs for their own perverted use, trying to blur the lines between Christianity and gangs. But being a Christian and being a gang member at the same time are opposites fighting for the same person.

So our discussions with Barry began to focus on the testing of personal faith. I reminded Barry that gang members would come at him and that his faith would correspondingly be tested. In one particular talk, I reminded Barry, "You know how God loves to test His people. Look at how Abraham was called to put his only son Isaac on the altar and sacrifice him as God commanded. And Abraham passed the test. God may allow gang members to come at you. People will be watching to see if you are really into the Word."

Barry did not appear to be worried, as he told me, "I'm ready for whatever it takes. I will follow the Lord every day because I know that He will always be there for me."

Since Barry already had prison experience, he was familiar with these kinds of issues. And the truth of it was that Barry seemed anxious to begin the time of testing so as to be able to prove his faith. All of this made it easier for Barry, Jim, and me. However, I sensed something deeper was going on here with the three of us. It first came out at the weekly prayer group that Jim and I attend with other pastors from the area. At these meetings we share joys, we unburden, and we pray. Our colleagues were generally aware of the work that Jim and I did at the jail. It was at one of these prayer group sessions that I admitted to our colleagues in ministry, "I'm not exactly sure if Jim would agree with me or not, but it's almost like Barry has become a child to me. It's going to be very difficult for me to say good-bye—especially knowing that he's going off to a dangerous place. It will be a place where his spiritual faith will come under fire constantly. Jim and I are about out of time with him. We have done as much as we can. I pray that it's been enough."

Physically, it was impossible for Barry to be my son since I am only seven years older than he is (though Jim has twenty-five years on him). Spiritually, it was definitely possible. Immediately, Jim spoke up at that prayer meeting to say that he agreed with me. It was as if Barry had become a son to him, too. None of us knew then, but the depth of that commitment was going to come into full force a couple of weeks later at the Union County Courthouse. At that moment of our heartfelt statements, we prayed for Barry. Then we prayed for the Ruby family, with special emphasis for Jane's daughter, Dana. During that prayer time, the Biblical connection came to me. I realized that Paul's letter to Philemon from the New Testament was being lived out in the time and space of all the moments we had with Barry. In Philemon, Paul meets the slave Onesimus. The slave goes through a spiritual transformation in prison under the direction of the Apostle Paul. When it is time for Onesimus to be sent home, Paul acknowledged that the slave had become like a child to him. The power of that revelation filled me with the Spirit. Our relationship with Barry had provided me with another moment of grace.

By October, Jim and I met with Barry together. We knew that not only were we sending Barry off like a sheep among wolves, but we would miss his hunger and thirst for the Good News. It was such a refreshing change from a world that is gripped by Christian apathy. We would also feel the void of his enjoyable company. The Barry who came into the Union County Jail was not the same Barry who was going out. In the same way, Onesimus returned to his master as a totally different person.

During these final sessions, I usually had my feet up against the bars, watching and listening to Barry and Jim talk about God. Barry had gotten his hair cut short in preparation for his trial. I noticed for the first time that he was kind of handsome, and that he had chubby cheeks. He and Jim would go back and forth fully engaged in the Biblical text at hand. They would talk to each other as if those vertical jail bars were not there, even though they were always between us. Sometimes they would ask me what I thought about a particular point, but I would often wave them off so as not to break the harmony of their discussion. Pastor Jim was usually tapping his black Bible on his knee during these encounters.

Still, against all of this, there was the matter of Barry's legal situation. The Union County Attorney's Office had offered him a plea bargain. If Barry would agree to the charge of second-degree murder, he would be eligible for parole after forty-two-and-one-half years. In addition, he would spare the families involved and the county the anguish of a trial. If Barry went to trial on the charge of first-degree murder, he would get fifty years without the possibility for parole. In either scenario, the courts would be bound by mandatory sentencing laws.

Jim and I had always told Barry that we would support his decisions about how he wanted to proceed with his case. After all, he was the one who was going to have to live with the consequences whatever they would be. Barry wanted to go to trial to, as he put it, to "tell his story." He wanted everyone to know that what happened was not a premeditated act. Barry said, "I deeply regret what had happened. I will regret it every day of my life. I think about it every day of my life and I pray about it every day of my life."

Barry said he had instructed his attorneys to prepare to go to trial. Yet, he told us, his attorneys wanted him to take the plea bargain. Outside of our meetings with Barry, Jim and I tried to understand the value of going to trial. We would sit at McDonald's sipping Diet Cokes, negating those with cheeseburgers, as we railed against mandatory sentencing laws. We consider these to be human folly because they remove the authority and compassion of judges from the drama. Jim made a decision on one of those fast-food excursions. He said, "We need to start a campaign to put an end to mandatory sentencing laws." Then he defiantly got up for a soda refill.

"Absolutely," I responded, though I knew in my heart of hearts that Jim and I had so much on our pastoral platters, that yet another battlefront would be just about impossible. Despite the formidable parameters of the laws of the state of Iowa, Jim and I decided we should write letters to the court on Barry's behalf. The letter I wrote is dated October 6, 2000. The text of that letter is as follows:

To whom it may concern,
I am writing this letter to you on behalf of Barry Chubick, Jr. Pastor Jim McCutchan of the Assembly of God Church here in Creston and I have been providing Barry with weekly spiritual counseling since his arrest several months ago.

As I have worked with Barry, I have seen considerable growth in his spiritual life as well as a genuine desire by him to embrace his Christian roots. I have also witnessed, in several of our meetings, a real and personal and painful remorse for the regrettable actions, which have led to his incarceration.

Given the above information, and based on my extensive experience with prison and jail ministry, it is my sincere appeal to you to apply compassion and mercy on behalf of Mr. Chubick. While the victims and the families in this case have suffered tremendously, our society will be better served with continued rehabilitation and healing grounded in compassion.

If I may be of any further help in this matter please feel free to contact me at any time.

Sincerely,
Rev. Terry Amann

The amazing thing was that Jim's letter was so close to mine that the court must have thought we wrote them together, but we didn't. Barry said his defense team told him the letters wouldn't mean anything for his case, but on the day we handed them to him, Barry's eyes filled with tears. I know he appreciated our honest concern.

What we decided, each time we chewed on Barry's legal situation was that Barry had nothing to gain by going to trial, and he had a lot to lose. We asked him question after question about all the avenues of each option, and we honored our commitment to support him. Then we would pray. Barry was determined with his decision. Then, right before the trial, he surprised us with the news that he had signed the plea bargain agreement. We read about the deal on Monday, October 9th, in the local newspaper, the *Creston News Advertiser*. Things had changed dramatically between Wednesday and Monday. Barry pleaded guilty to second-degree murder, which meant that he was going to have to serve the minimum forty-two-and-one-half year sentence.[13] What was a difficult issue, appeared to be settled. Barry, however, surprised the courtroom a couple of times, and the issue of the plea bargain would be one of those surprises.

11

A Time for Court

The god of this age has blinded the minds of unbelievers, so that they cannot see the light of the gospel of the glory of Christ, who is the image of God.

—2 Corinthians 4:4

I am truly very, very sorry and I will continue to pray for them every day of the rest of my life.

—Barry Chubick, Jr. in court.

It is now Thursday, November 9, 2000. It is the time of trial for Barry. His case is on the docket for 9:30 A.M. at the Union County Courthouse. I know the case will not start on time, but I arrive early anyway. This is a labor of love. On the previous Tuesday, I drove to Chicago on church business with the Rev. Pete Brantner. As we drove along Interstate 80 to the Windy City, we listened to the presidential election returns on the radio. We had only a few hours worth of work and left the city the next day at 3:00 P.M. Originally, we had planned to stay overnight and leave on Thursday morning. However, Barry's court date changed all that. Once again, we were back on Interstate 80 listening to more election coverage. Even with our interest in the bizarre election drama being broadcast to us on the radio, it was a long ride through the rain back to Creston. I got home about 1:00 A.M. By court time, I was very tired.

Jim comes into the court lobby from a side entrance at the same time I do. Like me, Jim is wearing a tan trench coat. We look more like FBI agents than ministers. Jim also appears very tired. He has been working several late nights because of an increase in illnesses and other ministerial challenges. We notice that these extra kinds of ministerial duties come and go in cycles. Jim has been trying to navigate through one of those cycles amidst an already busy schedule. He has a guest with him named Ray Sorensen. Ray is an evangelist, with a past that includes serious jail time. Ray's clothes are frumpy, and he is wearing tennis shoes. He has a baseball cap on that is turned slightly. Ray is an unlikely looking soldier in God's Army. Jim brought Ray to meet Barry on a couple of Wednesdays at the jail. Ray is here today as another source of spiritual support for Barry.

Jim reaches to shake my hand; "You made it back."

"Yeah," I reply. "It was tough with the rain and all, but I feel everything went well. This whole election stuff is something right out of the Twilight Zone. We did find some time to get some Chicago-style Pizza and some Dunkin' Donuts coffee." These are two luxuries from the city life that I sorely miss. Neither can be obtained in Creston. Since I had not been able to visit Barry the day before, I wonder if he is mentally prepared for what is about to take place. "Do you feel Barry is ready to roll with this today?"

Jim shrugs his shoulders, "We will just have to wait and see."

As we wait for court to begin, the lobby is filling up with people who are planning to attend the proceedings. Dana Ruby must be here, but neither Jim nor I know who she is. We meet Barry's cousin, Roxanne Carroll. She is one of those three cousins who have faithfully visited Barry on Wednesday afternoons after we were gone. Roxanne thanks Jim and me for helping Barry get through all of this. In turn, I thank her for also standing beside Barry. Many times I have seen family members disavow relatives once they learn that their next of kin is locked up behind bars.

Ray begins to talk with Roxanne about his own wild ride back from the brink of spiritual death and prison. She seems genuinely interested as Ray tells his tale. Watching Roxanne listen to Ray makes me think that over the last several months, she must have been a good listener for her cousin Barry, too. Barry's mother and father arrive. Jim and I meet them for the first time. Just like Roxanne, they both thank us for helping Barry. As his mother offers kind words to us, she cries.

At 10:35 A.M., court is finally called to order[14] with Union County District Court Judge, the Honorable David L. Christensen, presiding. I am struck by the irony of his name. Jim and Ray and I sit in the second row, in the middle of the courtroom. Barry is brought in. His ankles are locked together, but his arms are free. He is led to the defense table, and is seated between his two court-appointed attorneys, Todd Miler and Karen Emerson. Barry looks over to Jim and me, and gives us a worried smile.

Across the defense table from Barry, the state of Iowa is represented by Tim Kenyon, the Union County Attorney. Kenyon and I are both members of the local chapter of Rotary. This morning, we exchange a brief, professional glance. Kenyon and the state are assisted by Clinton Spurrier, from nearby Ringgold County.

As the formalities of opening the case are completed,

the judge informs a surprised court that papers have been filed, on behalf of Barry, to have his attorneys withdrawn from the case. Jim and I are learning of this development as it unfolds. A hush rises up through the court gallery. Barry's attorneys look down at the papers on the defense table in front of them. Barry is sworn in by the court so that he can speak to the issues at hand. The judge gives Barry the opportunity to speak. Barry addresses the court in a sad and quiet voice. He is not angry in any way, but frustration comes through. Barry tells the court that he was forced into the plea agreement.[15] I expect Judge Christensen to cut him off at any time, but he doesn't. The impact is that if Barry can replace his attorneys, he can also change his plea and go to trial. Thus, we are given yet another surprise.

As Barry talks and the formalities of legalese drone along, I can hear people weeping all around us. I am so tired. I begin to wonder how much Jim and I have accomplished with Barry. Has there been enough time for his Christian faith to take root? Could we have done more? And then a flood of memories takes over. I am listening to Barry talk to the judge, but I am seeing a kaleidoscope of images from the ten months. First there is the image of Barry each time we got up to leave on Wednesdays. He would put his face up against the bars and wrap his hands on the outside, clutching the bars with his elbows down. Sometimes he would say, "I love you guys." Always he would say, "I'll pray for you and your churches this week."

Then there is the memory of that precious Wednesday when the three of us shared Holy Communion. Jim brought the elements in a small travel kit. He set the elements on the television set that was a constant companion for Barry from the beginning of his incarceration.

Barry stood up against the bars while I stood on the other side of the television. When Jim spoke of the "precious blood of Jesus Christ that was shed for us and washed away our sins," I don't think there was a dry eye among the three of us. In that moment, our church consisted of the television set, the jail bars, the dim lighting, each other, and the mutual hope that was in our hearts. It was a place where two or more were gathered. . . .

I am checking back in with the court. Barry is still talking with the judge. The image is very powerful: Barry, standing on one side, chained at the feet, with nowhere to go. The judge on the other side of the courtroom, shrouded in a judicial robe, perched on the bench, the full weight of the law and Barry's fate in his hands. I make a conscious effort to go back to my memories in a desperate attempt to make sense of it all.

Now I remember our last two meetings together. Those two days come rushing upon me. When we finished our time together, Barry and I hugged each other through the cell bars. Neither one of us was sure which way to turn our heads as we leaned against the bars. We kind of laughed and cried as we pressed our cheeks against the cold steel. Then we squeezed as hard as we could. Our bodies were contorted as we tried to draw as close as possible to one another. We patted each other on the back with arms embraced under the watchful eye of the ceiling camera. Both of us had the imprints of the cell bars on our faces when we let go.

Finally, after a lengthy discussion, the judge denies Barry's request. He says, ". . . the application to have counsel, Mr. Miler and Ms. Emerson, withdrawn in representation of the defendant is denied."[16] This makes the issue of changing his plea a moot point. The judge rules that Barry is not "articulate"[17] in his reasons for dismissal. There were places where Barry wasn't forceful enough in his arguments. But after all, Barry isn't trained in the legal arena. All he can do is speak to what he understands fairness to be.

The next order of business is for Barry to give a statement to the court if he so desires. Judge Christensen asks Barry if he would like to say anything to the court. Barry answers in the affirmative. I am amazed at the peacefulness in his voice as Barry talks. The court has just rejected his legal request, and yet there isn't even a hint of anger or bitterness in his speech.

Then Barry surprises the courtroom proceedings again. He states that he would like someone else to speak on his behalf. "Could I have someone else state something for me, too, or just—is it just me or . . . ?"[18]

By the way the courtroom players are shifting around, it is obvious that this is an unusual request. Even the court reporter glances over at Barry. Judge Christensen announces that Barry will give a statement and then the court will allow him to name the person he wants to speak for him. All eyes are on Barry as he stands up and addresses the court. He does so with genuine remorse as he gives a moving apology for Jane's death and Dana's trauma. He tells the court, "I am truly very, very sorry. I will continue to pray for the family every day of the rest of my life, and I pray to God to comfort each and every one of them as He's comforted me through this ordeal. I am truly very deeply sorry. Thank you."[19]

The weeping around us increases as Barry speaks. At the conclusion of his statement, Barry sits down. The judge then asks him who will now speak for him. The prosecution team calls for a sidebar at the bench. All the attorneys approach the bench to confer with the judge. In the meantime, my first reaction is that Barry will have

Pastor Jim speak for him. I think back to that phone call with Dorie when Barry was looking for Jim. Based on that phone call, I am convinced that Jim is going to be asked. I start to silently pray for Jim, who is sitting directly to my right side. I don't know it yet, but Pastor Jim expects me to be called, so he is silently praying for me.

Five long minutes tick by. The lawyers return to their respective chairs as the judge announces that he will allow Barry to ask someone to say some words for him. Barry asks, "Terry Amann, brother, will you speak for me?"[20]

As Barry says this, he turns and points directly at me. Another hush whips through the courtroom. I am stunned by this request. I slowly stand up. I ask the judge if I may have permission to go around by the defense table. The judge grants the request. I walk around and go through the swinging gate that separates the gallery from the legal arena. Next, I walk over to stand by Barry, who has extended his hand to mine. I am not sure that Judge Christensen is going to allow me to touch Barry. We clasp hands as Barry looks up from the chair with eyes of friendship and thankfulness. He has tears in his eyes. Our months of divine grace together are being folded up and packed away, and there is no way to stop it. I stand over Barry's right shoulder, and I look directly at the judge.

Like Barry, I am not prepared with my words. Usually, I am quick on my feet. But on this day, I am fatigued and emotionally spent. Judge Christensen tells me to state my name. My statement to the court is slow and methodical. "Terry Amann, Presbyterian minister in Creston," I begin. "I've been out of town, and I didn't know that I was going to speak, Your Honor, so I guess I could speak from my heart. Myself and my colleague in ministry, Pastor Jim McCutchan, and I have been counseling Barry over the last ten months. I can tell you that many of those sessions were times Barry spent most of the time weeping for the events that occurred. There is great remorse in his heart for the victims in this case. And if anybody could go back and turn back the hands of time, it would be Barry Chubick. We know, Your Honor, that long incarceration in our society today is often brutal and unjust. I think Barry's going to do good things in his time. I think he'll use the time for rehabilitation. And so I would ask the court, once again, to use the wisdom of Solomon and to act with compassion. Thank you."[21]

Do my words change the outcome of the trial? They do not. Do my words bring comfort to Barry? At some level, they do. He told me later that at the point of the "hands of time," he really got choked up. Do these words bring peace to Dana and her family? This is an unknown that only God can really determine. Still, I pray that they do.

Barry Keith Chubick, Jr. is sentenced to fifty years behind bars for the stabbing death of Jane Ruby, and five years for the willful injury inflicted on Dana Ruby. He will have to serve a minimum of forty-two-and-one-half years before he is eligible for parole. Barry is also assessed almost $160,000 in restitution and legal fees. Then he is led away. The courtroom clears. I can still hear people crying. Jim and Ray and I go out into the lobby.

We decide Jim and I should see if Barry wants to talk. We move over toward the hallway door that separates the courthouse from the corridor leading to the jail. Barry's family is there, hugging each other. Jim walks over to Barry's father. I am leaning up against the wall in the hallway. Someone points out Dana to me. Jim and I have talked about meeting with her at some point, but ministerial demands just never really allowed it. Now I'm thinking that we really need to extend some kind of pastoral care to her, but at this moment in time, there just isn't anything left inside Jim or me to give. We are completely drained.

I look back over to where Jim is standing. He is grabbing Barry's father. Jim holds him by his arms and he says, "I'm sorry. If there's anything we can do . . . I, ah, I, ah, I just want to you to know . . . Barry is like a son to me. He's just like one of my boys!"

As he says this, Jim breaks out into full tears and pulls Barry Chubick, Sr. into a bear hug. Then Jim turns away with his head down and tears streaming down his face. I am leaning against the wall on one foot. My hands are in the pockets of my trench coat. Jim walks right past me and exits by way of the side door where he came in. I put my head back against the wall and take a deep breath. We have a Union County Ministerial Alliance meeting in a couple of minutes, a few blocks away. I know I'm not going to be in attendance, and I doubt Jim will make it either. Instead, I walk out of the crowded courthouse and drive home. My wife greets me at the door. She asks, "Well, how did it go?"

I tell her, "It was all just surreal. Just surreal." Then I go downstairs to the basement and collapse on the waterbed. I can't help but notice out the window that it is another very overcast day. Then sleep begins to take away my tears and my pain. . . .

12

Separation

The fear of the Lord is a fountain of life,
turning a man from the snares of death.
—Proverbs 14:27

I have also completed *Brothers in Blue* and a minister there was so astounded at how many verses I knew of Scripture while we were in the 'Catacombs' that he wanted me to write a letter to his seventh and eighth grade class on why memorizing Scripture is so important.
—Letter from prison by Barry Chubick, Jr.

Barry was sent away to prison soon after his day in court. He began serving his lengthy sentence in Oakdale, Iowa. Later he was transferred to the Fort Dodge Correctional Facility. Currently, Barry resides at the Newton Correctional Facility. With Barry gone, only time is left to determine the depth and the passion of his jailhouse conversion.

It wasn't too long before kites from Barry began to filter in to both Jim and me. I received a letter from Barry dated November 14, 2000. It was the last missive I got from Barry with the return address of the Union County Jail. In it, Barry told me his feelings after our final Wednesday together. Barry wrote: "I was sad because it would be our last time together for a while. But deep inside of me, as I was kneeling on the concrete floor and praying, I was swept over with joy. I couldn't stop smiling. I was praising the Lord and grinning from ear to ear. I tried and I just couldn't get the smile off of my face. I was afraid that the jailers would think I lost it. I was sad inside, but I was full of joy and confidence at the same time."

After a year and a half, Jim and I have a couple of stacks of letters from Barry. In each of these letters, there is a consistent theme of spiritual progression and search. His love of God and belief in the saving power of Jesus Christ is always close to his lips and his writing hand. According to Barry, he has had "Certificates just flowing in from Bible correspondence courses."

Barry has been moved to the prison in Newton, Iowa, so that he could participate in their *InnerChange Freedom Initiative (IFI)*. This is an intensive rehabilitation program grounded in Christian principles. It was founded by the Prison Fellowship Ministries of Charles W. Colson.[22] At Newton, Barry is a couple of hours away. Jim and I finally met with Barry face to face there one year after he had left Creston. It was an emotional reunion of three brothers in Christ.

Many times Barry and I talked about how God takes terrible situations and turns them for the good whenever God's people turn back to Him. There is no doubt in our minds that God is up to something through that "clay jar" named Barry, who holds the "treasure, which is the gospel."[23] Barry's passion for God is evident in all of his letters from prison. In addition to the *IFI* program, Barry is working towards a Bachelor's Degree in Theology.

Pastor Jim and I continue to minister at the Union County Jail on Wednesday afternoons. We have been joined by Susie Boyd, a Pentecostal pastor, who is a great help with the female inmates. Al Gates, a Deacon from First Baptist Church, is also part of what we now call *The God Squad.*

There are times when I talk with inmates and I wish they could meet Barry. Perhaps Barry's explanations of the Gospel could get through the walls of rebellion and drug abuse that dominate the lives of almost all the offenders we meet with. I must confess, though, there are other times when I feel like the current residents are occupying "Barry's cell."

So Jim and I scramble about trying to meet our church obligations and demands, at the same time, leaving our flocks to go over to the jail. There, we try to bring home the sheep who are lost. We still stop by McDonald's now and again. We seem to have trouble stealing time to go fishing at our favorite lake or to go for some occasional drives in the fast lane. We pray for Barry often. We watch as God uses him for His purposes. And we wonder how many other people, like Barry, are out there. People whom no one, including ourselves, is reaching with the Good News.

Pastor Jim and I lament, along with Barry Chubick, Jr., that Jane Ruby is dead. We feel sorrow for the trauma that Dana Ruby must live with. Both she and Barry would do anything to change the past that they share—but they can't. Barry's own words from court at his sentencing put this drama in perspective. He said, "There are no words of comfort. There are no words of comfort for the family. I've searched for them. I can't find them."[24]

So, in a broken world, we move forward with boldness—secure in the knowledge of the saving grace and forgiveness of Jesus Christ. We give thanks for this mysterious victory for the Cross. It is a victory that God brought about despite the tragedy that took place. It is a victory that began on a cold Wednesday in February, not very long ago. . . .

The work of ministering to those in jails and in prisons must go on so that they may come to know Christ. In Acts 2:21, a passage quoted from the prophet Joel sums up the ministerial task at hand: "And everyone who calls on the name of the Lord will be saved." Regrettably, churches and states do not want to spend the time or the money on prisoners. There are many more like Barry in prison—people whom God wants to reach—people who are ready to say "yes" to Jesus— people who can change. It is these words of Jesus from Luke 10:2 that ring true today: "The harvest is plentiful, but the workers are few." Thus, it is fitting that we close with this simple prayer: *May the Lord of the harvest send the laborers forth into the prison fields. Amen.*

Endnotes

1. All Biblical quotes have been taken from the *New International Version* of the Bible.
2. Philemon v. 11.
3. *"Man charged with murder," Creston News Advertiser;* Larry Peterson, pg. 1, Monday February 7, 2000. The same statistic is reported in: *"String of domestic violence deaths continue," Creston News Advertiser;* Stephani Finley, pg. 1, Monday February 7, 2000.
4. *"Chubick pleads not guilty;" Creston News Advertiser;* Larry Peterson, pg. 1, Friday, March 24, 2000.
5. *The Hymnbook,* published by the Presbyterian Church in the United States, The United Presbyterian Church in the U.S.A. and the Reformed Church in America; sixteenth printing, Richmond 1955.
6. Iowa government pamphlet, *Methamphetamine Labs: What Everyone Should Know;* Iowa Department of Public Health, Stephen C. Gleason, D.O., director.
7. Box, p. 38.
8. The names of people in this chapter have been changed to protect their identities.
9. *Good News Bible,* Today's English Version. American Bible Society, New York, 1976.
10. *The New King James* Version, Word Publishing, 1995.
11. JDM. P.O. Box 20149 New Orleans, Louisiana 70141–0149.
12. Acts 9:18.
13. *"Chubick pleads guilty," Creston News Advertiser;* Larry Peterson, pg. 1, Monday October 9, 2000.
14. Court transcript from the Iowa District Court for Union County; State of Iowa, *Plaintiff,* vs. *Barry Keith Chubick, Jr.,* Defendant; Lynne M. Hummel, CSR; pg. 1, line 10.
15. Ibid, pg. 4, lines 5–10.
16. Ibid, pg. 12, lines 12–14.
17. Ibid, p. 10, lines 17–21.
18. Ibid, p. 18, lines 5–7.
19. Ibid, p. 18, lines 20–25.

20. Ibid, p. 19, lines 20–21.
21. Ibid, p. 20, lines 1–17.
22. *"State and religion blend at prison,"* Des Moines Sunday Register; Juli Probasco-Sowers, pg. 1, Sunday April 1, 2001.
23. In Second Corinthians 4:7 the apostle Paul calls mortals "clay jars" who hold the "treasure," which is the gospel.
24. Court transcript from the Iowa District Court for Union County; State of Iowa, *Plaintiff*, vs. *Barry Keith Chubick, Jr.,* Defendant; Lynne M. Hummel, CSR; pg. 18, lines 21–25.

Bibliography

Albom, Mitch, *Tuesdays with Morrie;* New York, Doubleday, 1997.

Box, Steven, *Meth = Sorcery: Know the Truth;* Above All Ministry, Pierce City, MO.; Steven Box, copyright, 2001.

International Bible Society, *Holy Bible: New International Version*, East Brunswick, NJ, 1978.